GW01018138

COLL.

1

Collected Poems
1944-1949

Nelly Sachs

Translated by Michael Hamburger, Ruth and
Matthew Mead, and Michael Roloff
Introduction by Hans Magnus Enzensberger

GREEN INTEGER
KØBENHAVN & LOS ANGELES
2011

GREEN INTEGER BOOKS
Edited by Per Bregne
København / Los Angeles

Distributed in the United States by Consortium Book
Sales and Distribution, 1045 Westgate Drive, Suite 90
Saint Paul, Minnesota 55114-1065
Distributed in England and Europe by
Turnaround Publisher Services
Unit 3, Olympia Trading Estate
Coburg Road, Wood Green, London N22 6TZ
44 (0)20 88293009

(323) 857-1115 / http://www.greeninteger.com
Green Integer
6022 Wilshire Boulevard, Suite 200A
Los Angeles, California 90036 USA

First Green Integer Edition 2007
These poems were first published as
In den Wohnungendes Todes (Berlin: Aufbau-Verlag, 1947)
and *Sternverdunkelung* (Berlin: Suhrkamp Verlag, 1949)
Copyright © Shurkamp Verlag, Frankfurt am Main 1965
The English in this volume is reprinted, in different format, from
O The Chimneys: Selected Poems (New York: Farrar, Straus and Giroux, 1967)
Copyright ©1967 by Farrar, Straus and Giroux
and *The Seeker and Other Poems*
(New York: Farrar, Straus and Giroux, 1970)
Copyright ©1970 by Farrar, Straus and Giroux
Reprinted by agreement.
Back cover copy ©2011 by Green Integer

Design: Per Bregne
Typography: Kim Silva
Cover photograph: photograph of Nelly Sachs

LIBRARY OF CONGRESS CATALOGING IN PUBLICATION DATA
Nelly Sachs [1891-1970]
Collected Poems 1944-1949
ISBN: 978-1-933382-57-9
p. cm – Green Integer 181
I. Title II. Series III. Translators

Green Integer books are published for Douglas Messerli

Introduction

The oeuvre of Nelly Sachs is great and mysterious, two attributes that literary criticism has few occasions to apply to poetry these days. They are archaic attributes; let us define their meaning. Greatness has nothing to do with talent, and little to do with the bourgeois concept of genius that makes the creator unique among men and seeks to place him in the realm of the incomparable. The poet as superman, intellectual prince, Olympian, Titan belonged to the repertoire of the nineteenth century and passed away with it. Greatness has a more ancient heritage; it can be unobtrusive; it can neither be earned nor rewarded, least of all with the prizes our society is in a position to bestow: with success or "name." Greatness remains alien in the world, and the world cannot make better sense of it than in terms of fame, which itself is an archaic and almost obsolete response. Fame, quiet fame, has come to Nelly Sachs in recent years, late and unexpectedly. But as much as greatness is a mark of the person and not only of the work, one hesitates to claim greatness exclusively for her: on the contrary, her greatness is representative. It stands for others and their cause; out of her speaks more than herself. That cause remains indeterminate and nameless, however. And this indeterminateness has something to do with the mystery of her work, which is always, in Goethe's words, a manifest secret and not comparable to mystification or murky profundity.

The poems of Nelly Sachs are of this character: hard, but transparent. They do not dissolve in the weak solution of interpretations. Nor, at first, are they easy to read. One is in the habit of saying, usually as a reproach, about all modern poetry that it is difficult, as though this were a foregone conclusion; as if it were up to the authors to express themselves a little more obligingly. On this account it is often forgotten where the difficulty really lies. With Nelly Sachs the difficulty is never of a technical nature; she neither means to be calculating nor to shock; her poetry is neither a secret code nor a picture puzzle: what we are dealing with here are enigmas that do not add up when they are solved, but still retain an enigmatic aspect—and that aspect is what matters. Here interpretation can easily be overeager. The work demands of the reader not cleverness so much as humility: the work does not want to be made concrete or be transformed, but experienced, patiently and with exactness. Therefore, it should not be said what the work means; at most we can allow ourselves allusions, suggestions to show the reader the way—the possible way.

Gottfried Benn used to speak about his poems as though they could be understood one at a time, each one by itself—valuable "creations" which, if he was lucky, "were fit to survive," detached from any context and sufficient unto themselves. This is not so with Nelly Sachs's poetry, which is inconceivable as a series of individual artifacts. Since the appearance in 1946 of her first collection of poetry, *In the Habitations of Death*, she has been writing fundamentally a single book. The precedence of the whole over the individual in her work is not a formal characteristic; it does not express itself in an underlying structural law, in the composition as a cyclical or epic structure; it is more deeply rooted. This idea of *the book* that is the basis of her work is of religious origin. Beda Alleman, in his essay *Allusion to a Poetic Realm*, demonstrated that she has taken the Cabala as her model, especially *The Sohar*, a commentary on the Pentateuch.

> Then wrote the scribe of The Sohar
> opening the words' mesh of veins
> instilling blood from stars.

Thus begins a poem-sequence by Nelly Sachs which manifests the heritage that Alleman discusses. Book and inscription, archive and alphabet: these are concepts that recur throughout her work. They do not signify anything literary, but rather make literal use of the old concept of the book of nature, and, as it were, turn it around: the poetess does not copy nature's signs into her poems; she absorbs them so as to delineate future patterns:

> The alphabet's corpse rose from the grave,
> alphabet angel, ancient crystal,

immured by creation in drops of water
…
And unwraps, as though it were linen sheets
in which birth and death are swathed,
the alphabet womb, chrysalis
of green and red and white obscurity.

Nelly Sachs's book unfolds itself, gradually, with its language. Nothing in it is isolated; from one poem to the next the concrete detail is reiterated until its cosmic connotations are established. One of the varied images revealed throughout the book expresses this process itself: the image of the butterfly. The work itself is "alphabet's-corpse" and "chrysalis." This summer creature appears first in the early poem *Chorus of the Unborn*, though still in the form of a seemingly conventional simile, as a metaphor pure and simple:

We are caught
Like butterflies by the sentries of your
  yearning—

In a later poem from *And No One Knows How to Go On* the image is elaborated:

> All lands are ready to rise
> from the map…
> Ready to carry the last weight
> of melancholy in a suitcase, this chrysalis
> on the wings of which they will one day
> end their journey.

What has, as it were, been enclosed in this image from the very beginning liberates itself finally and enters one of the central themes of Nelly Sachs's work, the theme of metamorphosis:

> Fleeing,
> what a great reception
> on the way—
> …
> The sick butterfly
> will soon learn again of the sea—
> This stone
> with the fly's inscription
> gave itself into my hand—

> I hold instead of a homeland
> the metamorphoses of the world—

Not only the objects that appear in Nelly Sachs's book but even the words and images are subject to this law of transformation. For one of her most perfect poems. *Butterfly*, becomes both theme and title. This poem says:

> What lovely aftermath
> is painted in your dust.
> What royal sign
> in the secret of the air.

The image of the butterfly and the idea of creation as sign and inscription here combine with another basic word, which can be traced from the beginning to the end of her work: the word "dust." As an example of this, let us follow how one can read the word "dust" in this book, its course and its transformations from the first to the last poem.

At the beginning of this course stands not a metaphor but the black reality of our epoch. So the first poem of this book begins:

> O the chimneys
> On the ingeniously devised habitations of
>   death
> When Israel's body drifted as smoke
> Through the air—
> …
> O the chimneys!
> Freedom-way for Jeremiah and Job's dust—

Dust, ashes, smoke stand with terrible exactness and concreteness above the crematory ovens of the German concentration camps. This is the beginning that is asserted throughout all transformations of dust, which is never forgotten and is always part of the thought. It is handed on expressly in the poem *To You That Build the New House:*

> Oh, the walls and household utensils
> Are responsive as Aeolian harps
> Or like the field in which your sorrow grows,
> And they sense your kinship with dust,

Build, when the hourglass trickles,
But do not weep away the minutes
Together with the dust
That obscures the light.

Dust is also the sand in the hourglass; it becomes the image of transitoriness as such. Not human kind alone, the whole earth is dust, and all creatures with it; dust in which life leaves its impression, its sign, its inscription as a trace, which can be read from the wings of the butterfly like this image:

But who emptied your shoes of sand
When you had to get up, to die?
The sand which Israel gathered,
Its nomad sand?
Burning Sinai sand,
Mingled with throats of nightingales,
Mingled with wings of butterflies...

As sand the dust is at home in the desert, where, in otherwords, no shelter exists whatsoever. The home in the homelessness of the desert is baptized Israel. Nelly Sachs is the last poetess of Jewry who writes in German, and her work remains incomprehensible without this royal origin. In her Stockholm refuge she experienced the genocide of the Final Solution more closely than we who lived near the death camps, and her book remains the only poetic testimony that can hold its own beside the dumfounding horror of the documentary reports. As incomparable as this poetic deed may be, one cannot confine her work within this achievement. It is to do an injustice to this work if one seek to reduce it to this act of witnessing, to this lament, or even to supplying redeeming information for "overcoming" what no power can overcome.

To Nelly Sachs as to the ancient writings, Israel is representative of the story of all of creation's fortune and misfortune. Dust, smoke, ashes are not the "past," which one might be able to have done with, but are always contemporaneous. Today as well and every day it says:

The chimneys fly black flags
at the grave of air.

But man has said Ah
and climbs
a straight candle
into the night.

And even the stone partakes of the "metamor-
phoses of the world."

While the cricket scratches softly
at the invisible
and the stone dancing
changes its dust to music.

The path that this book traverses begins in flight
and ends as a *Journey into a Dustless Realm:* this is
the title of a later sequence of poems which the
poetess also used for the edition of her collected
poems. So palpable as the naked reality of the
ashes and smoke in the extermination camps, so
concretely begins the journey, as exile, dispos-
sessed banishment, flight from the henchmen of
1940 into peaceful Sweden, and like the dust this
journey ends as a cosmic one, as an image of the
world.

Inscription, butterfly, metamorphosis, flight: as these elements of her poetry unfold themselves and intertwine, so do all the words that stand in this book. Wherever the reader begins, with the metaphor of hair and fire, the hunter and the hunted, sea and wings, or finger and shoe: from every point the "words' mesh of veins" will open up to him, and even the most daring telescoping of expression, the cryptically condensed stanza will become transparent to him when he traces the multifariousness of this coral reef of images. This poetry is also cabalistic in this linguistic sense: as the work of a magical *ars combinatora* that knows how to grasp even the incommensurable ever more lightly the more remote it is.

So this "royal word written far away" ought to become readable even if the book,

> This chain of enigmas
> hung on the neck of night,

will maintain its manifest secret against everyone who reads it, and thus will live on.

—MARCH 1963

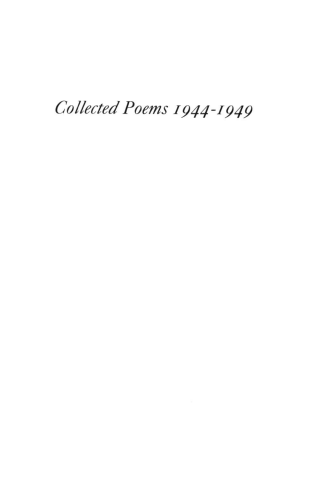

Collected Poems 1944-1949

In den Wohnungen des Tods (1947)

In the Habitations of Death

For my dead brothers and sisters

O die Schornsteine

Und wenn diese meine Haut zerschlagen sein
wird, so werde ich ohne mein Fleisch Gott
schauen.—HIOB

O die Schornsteine
Auf den sinnreich erdachten Wohnungen des Todes,
Als Israels Leib zog aufgelöst in Rauch
Durch die Luft—
Als Essenkehrer ihn ein Stern empfing
Der schwarz wurde
Oder war es ein Sonnenstrahl?

O die Schornsteine!
Freiheitswege für Jeremias und Hiobs Staub—
Wer erdachte euch und baute Stein auf Stein
Den Weg für Flüchtlinge aus Rauch?

O the chimneys

And though after my skin worms destroy this
body, yet in my flesh shall I see God.
—JOB, 19:26

O the chimneys
On the ingeniously devised habitations of death
When Israel's body drifted as smoke
Through the air—
Was welcomed by a star, a chimney sweep,
A star that turned black
Or was it a ray of sun?

O the chimneys!
Freedomway for Jeremiah and Job's dust—
Who devised you and laid stone upon stone
The road for refugees of smoke?

O die Wohnungen des Todes,
Einladend hergerichtet
Für den Wirt des Hauses, der sonst Gast war—
O ihr Finger,
Die Eingangsschwelle legend
Wie ein Messer zwischen Leben und Tod—

O ihr Schornsteine,
O ihr Finger,
Und Israels Leib im Rauch durch die Luft!

O the habitations of death,
Invitingly appointed
For the host who used to be a guest—
O you fingers
Laying the threshold
Like a knife between life and death—

O you chimneys,
O you fingers
And Israel's body as smoke through the air!

—Translated by Michael Roloff

An euch, die das neue Haus bauen

Es gibt Steine wie Seelen.—RABBI NACHMAN

Wenn du dir deine Wände neu aufrichtest—
Deinen Herd, Schlafstatt, Tisch und Stuhl—
Hänge nicht deine Tränen um sie, die dahingegangen,
Die nicht mehr mit dir wohnen werden
An den Stein
Nicht an das Holz—
Es weint sonst in deinen Schlaf hinein,
Den kurzen, den du noch tun musst.

Seufze nicht, wenn du dein Laken bettest,
Es mischen sich sonst deine Träume
Mit dem Schweiss der Toten.

Ach, es sind die Wände und die Geräte
Wie die Windharfen empfänglich
Und wie ein Acker, darin dein Leid wächst,
Und spüren das Staubverwandte in dir.

24

To you that build the new house

"There are stones like souls"—RABBI NACHMAN

When you come to put up your walls anew—
Your stove, your bedstead, table and chair—
Do not hang your tears for those who departed,
Who will not live with you then,
On to the stone.
Nor on the timber—
Else weeping will pierce the sleep,
The brief sleep you have yet to take.

Do not sigh when you bed your sheets,
Else your dreams will mingle
With the sweat of the dead.

Oh, the walls and household utensils
Are responsive as Aeolian harps
Or like a field in which your sorrow grows,
And they sense your kinship with dust.

Baue, wenn die Stundenuhr rieselt,
Aber weine nicht die Minuten fort
Mit dem Staub zusammen,
Der das Licht verdeckt.

Build, when the hourglass trickles,
But do not weep away the minutes
Together with the dust
That obscures the light.

—Translated by Michael Hamburger

O der weinenden Kinder Nacht!

O der weinenden Kinder Nacht!
Der zum Tode gezeichneten Kinder Nacht!
Der Schlaf hat keinen Eingang mehr.
Schreckliche Wärterinnen
Sind an die Stelle der Mütter getreten,
Haben den falschen Tod in ihre Handmuskeln
   gespannt,
Säen ihn in die Wände und ins Gebälk—
Überall brütet es in den Nestern des Grauens.
Angst säugt die Kleinen statt der Muttermilch.

Zog die Mutter noch gestern
Wie ein weisser Mond den Schlaf heran,
Kam die Puppe mit dem fortgeküssten Wangenrot
In den einen Arm,
Kam das ausgestopfte Tier, lebendig
In der Liebe schon geworden,
In den andern Arm,—
Weht nun der Wind des Sterbens,
Bläst die Hemden über die Haare fort,
Die niemand mehr kämmen wird.

O the night of the weeping children!

O the night of the weeping children!
O the night of the children branded for death!
Sleep may not enter here.
Terrible nursemaids
Have usurped the place of mothers,
Have tautened their tendons with the false death,
Sow it on to the walls and into the beams—
Everywhere it is hatched in the nests of horror.
Instead of mother's milk, panic suckles those
   little ones.

Yesterday Mother still drew
Sleep toward them like a white moon,
There was the doll with cheeks derouged by kisses
In one arm,
The stuffed pet, already
Brought to life by love,
In the other—
Now blows the wind of dying,
Blows the shifts over the hair
That no one will comb again.

    —Translated by Michael Hamburger

Wer aber leerte den Sand aus euren Schuhen

Wer aber leerte den Sand aus euren Schuhen,
Als ihr zum Sterben aufstehen musstet?
Den Sand, den Israel heimholte,
Seinen Wandersand?
Brennenden Sinaisand,
Mit den Kehlen von Nachtigallen vermischt,
Mit den Flügeln des Schmetterlings vermischt,
Mit dem Sehnsuchtsstaubder Schlangen vermischt,
Mit allem was abfiel von der Weisheit
    Salomos vermischt
Mit dem Bitteren aus des Wermuts
    Geheimnis vermischt—

O ihr Finger,
Die ihr den Sand aus Totenschuhen leertet,
Morgen schon werdet ihr Staub sein
In den Schuhen Kommender!

But who emptied your shoes of sand

But who emptied your shoes of sand
When you had to get up, to die?
The sand which Israel gathered,
Its nomad sand?
Burning Sinai sand,
Mingled with throats of nightingales,
Mingled with wings of butterflies,
Mingled with the hungry dust of serpents;
Mingled with all that fell from the wisdom of Solomon,
Mingled with what is bitter in the mystery
 of wormwood—

O you fingers
That emptied the deathly shoes of sand.
Tomorrow you will be dust
In the shoes of those to come.

—*Translated by Michael Hamburger*

Auch der Greise

Auch der Greise
Letzten Atemzug, der schon den Tod anblies
Raubtet ihr noch fort.
Die leere Luft,
Zitternd vor Erwartung, den Seufzer der Erleichterung
Zu erfüllen, mit dem diese Erde fortgestossen wird—
Die leere Luft habt ihr beraubt!

Der Greise
Ausgetrocknetes Auge
Habt ihr noch einmal zusammengepresst
Bis ihr das Salz der Verzweiflung gewonnen hattet—
Alles was dieser Stern
An Krümmungen der Qual besitzt,
Alles Leiden aus den dunklen Verliesen der Würmer
Sammelte sich zuhauf—

O ihr Räuber von echten Todesstunden,
Letzten Atemzügen und der Augenlider *Gute Nacht*
Eines set euch gewiss:

Even the old men's last breath

Even the old men's last breath
That had already grazed death
You snatched away.
The empty air
Trembling
To fill the sigh of relief
That thrusts this earth away—
You have plundered the empty air!

The old men's
Parched eyes
You pressed once more
Till you reaped the salt of despair—
All that this star owns
Of the contortions of agony,
All suffering from the dungeons of worms
Gathered in heaps—

O you thieves of genuine hours of death,
Last breaths and the eyelids' *Good Night*
Of one thing be sure:

Es sammelt der Engel ein
Was ihr fortwarft,
Aus der Greise verfrühter Mitternacht
Wird sich ein Wind der letzten Atemzüge auftun,
Der diesen losgerissenen Stern
In seines Herrn Hände jagen wird!

The angel, it gathers
What you discarded,
From the old men's premature midnight
A wind of last breaths shall arise
And drive this unloosed star
Into its Lord's hands!

—*Translated by Michael Roloff*

Ein totes Kind spricht

Die Mutter hielt mich an der Hand.
Dann hob Jemand das Abschiedsmesser:
Die Mutter löste ihre Hand aus der meinen,
Damit es mich nicht träfe.
Sie aber berührte noch einmal leise meine Hüfte—
Und da blutete ihre Hand—

Von da ab schnitt mir das Abschiedsmesser
Den Bissen en der Kehle entzwei—
Es fuhr in der Morgendämmerung mit der Sonne hervor
Und begann, sich in meinen Augen zu schärfen—
In meinem Ohr schliffen sich Winde und Wasser,
Unde jede Trostesstimme stach in mein Herz—

Als man mich zum Tode führte,
Fühlte ich im letzten Augenblick noch
Das Herausziehen des grossen Abschiedsmessers.

A dead child speaks

My mother held me by my hand.
Then someone raised the knife of parting:
So that it should not strike me,
My mother loosed her hand from mine.
But she lightly touched my thighs once more
And her hand was bleeding—

After that the knife of parting
Cut in two each bite I swallowed—
It rose before me with the sun at dawn
And began to sharpen itself in my eyes—
Wind and water ground in my ear
And every voice of comfort pierced my heart—

As I was led to death
I still felt in the last moment
The unsheathing of the great knife of parting.

—Translated by Ruth and Matthew Mead

Einer war, der blies den Schofar

Und das Sinken geschieht
um des Steigens willen
—BUCH SOHAR

Einer war,
Der blies den Schofar—
Warf nach hinten das Haupt,
Wie die Rehe tun, wie die Hirsche
Bevor sie trinken an der Quelle.
Bläst:
Tekia
Ausfährt der Tod im Seufzer—
Schewarim
Das Samenkorn fällt—
Terua
Die Luft erzählt von einem Licht!
Die Erde kreist und die Gestirne kreisen
Im Schofar,
Den Einer bläst—
Und um den Schofar brennt der Tempel—

Someone blew the Shofar

*The sinking occurs for the sake
of the rising*
—BOOK OF SOHAR

Someone
Blew the Shofar—
Threw back his head
As the deer do, as the stags
Before they drink at the spring.
Blows
Tekiah   — Sounds
Death departs in the sigh—
Shewarim
The seed descends—
Terua
The air tells of a light!
The earth circles and the constellations circle
In the Shofar
Which someone blows—
And round the Shofar the temple burns—

Und Einer bläst—
Und um den Schofar stürzt der Tempel—
Und Einer bläst—
Und um den Schofar ruht die Asche—
Und Einer bläst—

And someone blows—
And round the Shofar the temple falls—
And someone blows—
And round the Shofar the ashes rest—
And someone blows—

—Translated by Ruth and Matthew Mead

Hände

Hände
Der Todesgärtner,
Die ihr aus der Wiegenkamille Tod,
Die auf den harten Triften gedeiht
Oder am Abhang,
Das Treibhausungeheuer eures Gewerbes gezüchtet
   habt.
Hände,
Des Leibes Tabernakel aufbrechend,
Der Geheimnisse Zeichen wie Tigerzähne packend—
Hände,
Was tatet ihr,
Als ihr de Hände von kleinen Kindern waret?
Hieltet ihr eine Mundharmonika, die Mähne
Eines Schaukelpferdes, fasstet der Mutter Rock im
   Dunkel,
Zeigtet auf ein Wort im Kinderlesebuch—
War es Gott vielleicht, oder Mensch?

Hands

Hands
of the gardeners of death,
you who have grown the greenhouse monster of
   your trade
from the cradle camomile death
which thrives on the hard pastures
or on the slope.
Hands
breaking open the tabernacle of the body,
gripping the signs of the mysteries like tiger's teeth—
Hands,
what did you do
when you were tiny children's hands?
Did you hold a mouth organ, the mane
of a rocking horse, clutch your mother's skirt in the dark,
did you point to a word in a reading book—
Was it God perhaps, or Man?

Ihr wügenden Hände,
War eure Mutter tot,
Eure Frau, euer Kind?
Dass ihr nur noch den Tod in den Händen hieltet,
In den wügenden Händen?

You strangling hands,
was your mother dead,
your wife, your child?
So that all that you held in your hands was death,
in your strangling hands?

　—Translated by Ruth and Matthew Mead

Schon vom Arm des himmlisch
en Trostes umfangen

Schon vom Arm des himmlischen Trostes umfangen
Steht die wahnsinnige Mutter
Mit den Fetzen ihres zerrissenen Verstandes,
Mit den Zundern ihres verbrannten Verstandes
Ihr totes Kind einsargend,
Ihr verlorenes Licht einsargend,
Ihre Hände zu Krügen biegend,
Aus der Luft füllend mit dem Leib ihres Kindes,
Aus der Luft füllend mit seinen Augen, seinen Haaren
Und seinem flatternden Herzen—

Dann küsst sie das Luftgeborene
Und stirbt!

Already embraced by the arm
of heavenly solace

Already embraced by the arm of heavenly solace
The insane mother stands
With the tatters of her torn mind
With the charred tinders of her burnt mind
Burying her dead child,
Burying her lost light,
Twisting her hands into urns,
Filling them with the body of her child from the air,
Filling them with his eyes, his hair from the air,
And with his fluttering heart—

Then she kisses the air-born being
And dies!

—*Translated by Michael Roloff*

Welche geheimen Wünsche des Blutes

Welche geheimen Wünsche des Blutes,
Träume des Wahnes und tausendfach
Gemordetes Erdreich
Liessen den schrecklichen Marionettenspieler
   entstehen?

Er, der mit schäumendem Munde
Furchtbar umblies
Die runde, kreisende Bühne seiner Tat
Mit dem aschgrau ziehenden Horizont der Angst!

O die Staubhügel, die, wie von bösem Mond gezogen
Die Möder spielten:

Arme auf und ab,
Beine auf und ab
Und die untergehende Sonne des Sinaivolkes
Als den roten Teppich under den Füssen.

What secret cravings of the blood

What secret cravings of the blood,
Dreams of madness and earth
A thousand times murdered,
Brought into being the terrible puppeteer?

Him who with foaming mouth
Dreadfully swept away
The round, the circling state of his deed
With the ash-gray, receding horizon of fear?

O the hills of dust, which as though drawn by an
   evil moon
The murderers enacted:

Arms up and down,   *movement*
Legs up and down
And the setting sun of Sinai's people
A red carpet under their feet.

Arme auf und ab,
Beine auf und ab
Und am ziehenden aschgrauen Horizont der Angst
Risengross das Gestirn des Todes
Wie die Uhr der Zeiten stehend.

Arms up and down,
Legs up and down
And on the ash-gray receding horizon of fear
Gigantic the constellation of death
That loomed like the clock face of ages.

—*Translated by Michael Hamburger*

Lange haben wir das Lauschen verlernt!

Ehe es wächst, lasse ich euch es erlauschen
JESAIA

Lange haben wir das Lauschen verlernt!
Hatte Er uns gepflanzt einst zu lauschen
Wie Dünengras gepflanzt, am ewigen Meer,
Wollten wir wachsen auf feisten Triften,
Wie Salat im Hausgarten stehn.

Wenn wir auch Geschäfte haben,
Die weit fort führen
Von Seinem Licht,
Wenn wir auch das Wasser aus Röhren trinken,
Und es erst sterbend naht
Unserem ewig dürstenden Mund—
Wenn wir auch auf einer Strasse schreiten,
Darunter die Erde zum Schweigen gebracht wurde
Von einem Pflaster,
Verkaufen dürfen wir nicht unser Ohr,
O, nicht unser Ohr dürfen wir verkaufen.

How long have we forgotten how to listen!

Before they spring forth I tell you of them
ISAIAH 42:9

How long have we forgotten how to listen!
He planted us once to listen
Planted us like lyme grass by the eternal sea,
We wanted to grow on fat pastures,
To stand like lettuce in the kitchen—garden.

Although we have business
That leads us far
From his light,
Although we drink tap water,
And only as it dies it reaches
Our eternally thirsting mouths—
Although we walk down a street
Beneath which earth has been silenced
By a pavement,
We must not sell our ears,
Oh, we must not sell our ears.

Auch auf dem Markte,
Im Errechnen des Staubes,
Tat manch einer schnell einen Sprung
Auf der Sehnsucht Seil,
Weil er etwas hörte,
Aus dem Staube heraus tat er den Sprung
Und sättigte sein Ohr.
Presst, o presst an der Zerstörung Tag
An die Erde das lauschende Ohr,
Und ihr werdet hören, durch den Schlaf hindurch
Werdet ihr hören
Wie im Tode
Das Leben beginnt.

Even in the market,
In the computation of dust,
Many had made a quick leap
Onto the tightrope of longing,
Because they heard something,
And leapt out of the dust
And sated their ears.
Press, oh press on the day of destruction
The listening ear to the earth,
And you will hear, through your sleep
You will hear
How in death
Life begins.

—*Translated by Ruth and Matthew Mead*

Ihr Zuschauenden

Unter deren Blicken getötet wurde.
Wie man auch einen Blick im Rücken fühlt,
So fühlt ihr an euerm Leibe
Die Blicke der Toten.

Wieviel brechende Augen werden euch ansehn
Wenn ihr aus den Verstecken ein Veilchen
   pflückt?
Wieviel flehend erhobene Hände
In dem märtyrerhaft geschlungenen Gezweige
Der alten Eichen?
Wieviel Erinnerung wächst im Blute
Der Abendsonne?

O die ungesungenen Wiegenlieder
In der Turteltaube Nachtruf—
Manch einer hätte Sterne herunterholen können,
Nun muss es der alte Brunnen für ihn tun!

You onlookers

Whose eyes watched the killing.
As one feels a stare at one's back
You feel on your bodies
The glances of the dead.

How many dying eyes will look at you
When you pluck a violet from its hiding place?
How many hands be raised in supplication
In the twisted martyr-like branches
Of old oaks?
How much memory grows in the blood
Of the evening sun?

O the unsung cradlesongs
In the night cry of the turtledove—
Many a one might have plucked stars from the sky
Now the old well must do it for them!

Ihr Zuschauenden,
Die ihr keine Mörderhand erhobt,
Aber die ihr den Staub nicht von eurer Sehnsucht
Schütteltet,
Die ihr stehenbliebt, dort, wo er zu Licht
Verwandelt wird.

You onlookers,
You who raised no hand in murder,
But who did not shake the dust
From your longing,
You who halted there, where dust is changed
To light.

—*Translated by Ruth and Matthew Mead*

Lange schon fielen die Schatten

Lange schon fielen die Schatten.
Nicht sind gemeint jetzt
Jene lautlosen Schläge der Zeit
Die den Tod füllen—
Des Lebensbaumes abgefallene Blätter—

Die Schatten des Schrecklichen fielen
Durch das Glas der Träume,
Von Daniels Deuterlicht erhellt.

Schwarzer Wald wuchs erstickend um Israel,
Gottes Mitternachtssängerin.
Sie verging im Dunkeln,
Namenlos geworden.

O ihr Nachtigallen in allen Wäldern der Erde!
Gefiederte Erben des toten Volkes,
Wegweiser der gebrochenen Herzen,
Die ihr euch füllt am Tage mit Tränen,
Schluchzet es aus, schluchzet es aus
Der Kehle schreckliches Schweigen vor dem Tod.

The shadows fell long ago

The shadows fell long ago.
Here are not meant
Those silent strokes of time
That fill death—
Fallen leaves of the tree of life—

The shadows of terror fell
Through the glass of dreams,
Lit by the prophetic light of Daniel.

Black forest grew suffocatingly round Israel,
God's midnight singer.
She perished in darkness,
Her name lost.

O you nightingales in all the woods of earth!
Plumed heirs of a dead people,
Signpost of broken hearts,
You who fill yourselves by day with tears,
Sob out, sob out
The throat's terrible silence before death.

—Translated by Ruth and Matthew Mead

Die Kerze, die ich für dich entzümdet habe

Die Kerze, die ich für dich entzündet habe,
Spricht mit der Luft der Flammensprache Beben,
Und Wasser tropft vom Auge; aus dem Grabe
Dein Staub vernehmlich ruft zum ewgen Leben.

O hoher Treffpunkt in der Armut Zimmer.
Wenn ich nur wüsste, was die Elemente meinen;
Sie deuten dich, denn alles deutet immer
Auf dich; ich kann nichts tun als weinen.

Talking to air in words of flame

Talking to air in words of flame that leap and wave
The candle I have lit for you burns tall,
Water drips from my eye; out of the grave
Your dust calls clearly to the life eternal.

O high encounter in the room of need.
If I but knew what the elements intend;
They define you, for everything indeed
Always defines you; my tears never end.

—Translated by Ruth and Matthew Mead

Nacht, mein Augentrost

Nacht, mein Augentrost du, ich habe meinen Geliebten
   verloren!
Sonne, du trägst sein Blut in deinem Morgen-und
   Abend-gesicht.
O mein Gott, wird wo auf Erden ein Kind
   jetzt geboren,
Lass es nicht zu, dass sein Herz vor der blutenden
   Sonne zerbricht.

Mörder, aus welchem Grabstaub warst du einmal so
   schrecklich bekleidet?
Trug ihn ein Wind von einem Stern, den ein
   Nachtmahr behext
Wie Totenschnee hinab auf eine Schar, die sich zu
   Gott hindurchleidet,
Mörder, an deinen Händen zehnfacher
   Marterpfahl wächst.

Night, my euphrasy

Night, my euphrasy, I have lost my beloved!
Sun, you bear his blood in your face at dawn and when
   day is done.
Wherever on earth a child is being born now,
   O God,
Do not allow its heart to break at the sight of the
   bleeding sun.

Murderer, in what sepulchral dust were you once
   so grimly clad?
Was it borne from a star bewitched by a
   nightmare, falling like the snow
That falls from the dead upon the throng which
   suffers its way to God,
Murderer upon whose hands ten stakes of torture grow.

Darum auch spürtest du nicht der Liebe Zittern
 im Morden,
Da sie ein letztes Mal aus soviel Küssen
 dich angehaucht—
Darum ist ihr, der Hiobzerschlagenen, keine
 Antwort geworden,
Die dich zu Ihm wieder, zu Ihm wieder, hätte
 untergetaucht!

So that you did not feel the quiver of love as
  you murdered,
When the final kiss of so many kisses they breathed
  at you in pain—
So that she who was smitten like Job received no
  answering word,
Which would have immersed you again in Him,
  in Him again!

—*Translated by Ruth and Matthew Mead*

Vielleicht aber braucht Gott die Sehnsucht

Vielleicht aber braucht Gott die Sehnsucht, wo sollte
  sonst sie auch bleiben,
Sie, die mit Küssen and Tränen und Seufzern füllt die
  geheimnisvollen Räume der Luft—
Vielleicht ist sie das unsichtbare Erdreich, daraus die
  glühenden Wurzeln der Sterne treiben—
Und die Strahlenstimme über die Felder der Trennung,
  die zum Wiedersehn ruft?
O mein Geliebter, vielleicht hat unsere Liebe in den
  Himmel der Sehnsucht schon Welten geboren—
Wie unser Atemzug, ein—und aus, baut eine Wiege für
  Leben und Tod?
Sandkörner wir beide, dunkel vor Abschied, und in das
  goldene Geheimnis der Geburten verloren,
Und vielleicht schon von kommenden Sternen,
  Monden und Sonnen umloht.

But perhaps God needs the longing

But perhaps God needs the longing, wherever else
   should it dwell,
Which with kisses and tears and sighs fills mysterious
   spaces of air—
And perhaps is invisible soil from which roots of stars
   grow and swell—
And the radiant voice across fields of parting which calls
   to reunion there?
O my beloved, perhaps in the sky of longing worlds
   have been born of our love—
Just as our breathing, in and out, builds a cradle for life
   and death?
We are grains of sand, dark with farewell, lost in births'
   secret treasure trove
Around us already perhaps future moons, suns and stars
   blaze in a fiery wreath.

—Translated by Ruth and Matthew Mead

Auch dir, du mein Geliebter

Auch dir, du mein Geliebter,
Haben zwei Hände, zum Darreichen geboren,
Die Schuhe abgerissen,
Bevor sie dich töteten.
Zwei Hände, die sich darreichen müssen
Wenn sie zu Staub zerfallen.
Deine Schuhe waren aus einer Kalbshaut.
Wohl waren sie gegerbt, gefärbt,
Der Pfriem hatte sie durchstochen—
Aber wer weiss, wo noch ein letzter lebendiger
Hauch wohnt?
Während der kurzen Trennung
Zwischen deinem Blut und der Erde
Haben sie Sand hineingespart wie eine Stundenuhr
Die jeden Augenblick Tod füllt.
Deine Füsse!
Die Gedanken eilten ihnen voraus.
Die so schnell bei Gott waren,
So warden deine Füsse müde,
Wurden wund urn dein Herz einzuholen.

Two hands, born to give

Two hands, born to give,
Tore off your shoes
My beloved,
Before they killed you.
Two hands, which will have to give themselves up
When they turn to dust.
Your shoes were made of calfskin.
They were well tanned and dyed,
The awl had pierced them—
But who knows where a last living breath
Still dwells?
During the short parting
Between your blood and earth
They trickled sand like an hourglass
Which fills each moment with death.
Your feet!
The thoughts sped before them.
They came so quickly to God
That your feet grew weary,
Grew sore in trying to catch up with your heart.

Aber die Kalbshaut,
Darüber einmal die warme leckende Zunge
Des Muttertieres gestrichen war,
Ehe sie abgezogen wurde—
Wurde noch einmal abgezogen
Von deinen Füssen,
Abgezogen—
O du mein Geliebter!

But the calfskin
That the warm licking tongue
Of the mother-cow once stroked
Before the skin was stripped—
Was stripped once more
From your feet,
Torn off—
O my beloved!

—*Translated by Ruth and Matthew Mead*

Du gedenkst der Fusspur

Alles Vergessnen gedenkst du von Ewigkeit her

Du gedenkst der Fusspur, die sich mit Tod füllte
Bei dem Annahen des Häschers.
Du gedenkst der bebenden Lippen des Kindes
Als sie den Abschied von seiner Mutter
    erlernen mussten.
Du gedenkst der Mutterhände, die ein
    Grab aushöhlten
Für das an ihrer Brust Verhungerte.
Du gedenkst der geistesverlorenen Worte,
Die eine Braut in die Luft hineinredete zu ihrem
    toten Bräutigam.

You remember the footprint

All that is forgotten you remember from eternity

You remember the footprint which filled with death
As the myrmidon approached.
You remember the child's trembling lips
As they had to learn their farewell to their mother.
You remember the mother's hands which scooped
  out a grave
For the child which had starved at her breast.
You remember the mindless words
That a bride spoke into the air to her dead bridegroom.

—*Translated by Ruth and Matthew Mead*

Qual, Zeitmesser eines fremden Sterns

Die Gewänder des Morgens sind nicht
die Gewänder des Abends.—BUCH SOHAR

Qual, Zeitmesser eines fremden Sterns,
Jede Minute mit anderem Dunkel färbend—
Qual deiner erbrochenen Tür,
Deines erbrochenen Schlafes,
Deiner fortgehenden Schritte,
Die das letzte Leben hinzählten,
Deiner zertretenen Schritte,
Deiner schleifenden Schritte,
Bis sie aufhörten Schritte zu sein für mein Ohr.
Qual urn das Ende deiner Schritte
Vor einem Gitter,
Dahinter die Flur unserer Sehnsucht zu
    wogen begann—
O Zeit, die nur nach Sterben rechnet,
Wie leicht wird Tod nach dieser langen Übung sein.

Agony, metronome of an alien star

The robes of morning are not
the robes of evening.—THE SOHAR

Agony, metronome of an alien star,
Staining each minute with a different darkness—
Agony of your broken door,
Your broken sleep,
Your departing steps
That counted out the remains of life,
Of your crushed steps,
Your dragging steps,
Till they ceased being steps to my ear.
Agony of the end of your steps
Before an iron grate
Behind which the meadow of our yearning
   began to sway—
O time whose only measurement is dying,
How easy death will be after this long rehearsal.

—Translated by Michael Roloff

Ich sah erne Stelle

Ich sah erne Stelle, wo ein Herd stand—
Auch fand ich einen Männerhut—
O, mein Geliebter, welcher Sand
Weiss um dein Blut?

Die Schwelle, die liegt ohne Tür
Sie liegt zum Beschreiten bereit—
Dein Haus, mein Geliebter, ich spür
Ist ganz von Gott verschneit.

I found a hat

I found a hat a man had worn—
Saw where a stove had stood—
What sand, O my beloved,
Knows of your blood?

The threshold lies without a door
Lies waiting to be trod—
The house of him whom I adore
Is all snowed in by God.

—Translated by Ruth and Matthew Mead

Im Morgengrauen

Im Morgengrauen,
Wenn ein Vogel das Erwachen übt—
Beginnt die Sehnsuchtsstunde allen Staubes
Den der Tod verliess.

O Stunde der Geburten,
Kreissend in Qualen, darin sich die erste Rippe
Eines neuen Menschen bildet.

Geliebter, die Sehnsucht deines Staubes
Zieht brausend durch mein Herz.

In the gray dawn

In the gray dawn
When a bird practices awakening—
Begins the hour of longing for all dust
That death deserted.

O hour of births,
Laboring in torments, in which the first rib
Of a new man forms.

Beloved, the longing of your dust
Moves roaring through my heart.

—*Translated by Ruth and Matthew Mead*

Wenn ich nur wüßte

Wenn ich nur wüsste,
Worauf dein letzter Blick ruhte.
War es ein Stein, der schon viele letzte Blicke
Getrunken hatte, bis sie in Blindheit
Auf den Blinden fielen?

Oder war es Erde,
Genug, urn einen Schuh zu füllen,
Und schon schwarz geworden
Von soviel Abschied
Und von soviel Tod bereiten?

Oder war es dein letzter Weg,
Der dir das Lebewohl von allen Wegen brachte
Die du gegangen warst?

Eine Wasserlache, ein Stück spiegelndes Metall,
Vielleicht die Gürtelschnalle deines Feindes,
Oder irgend ein anderer, kleiner Wahrsager
Des Himmels?

If I only knew

If I only knew
On what your last look rested.
Was it a stone that had drunk
So many last looks that they fell
Blindly upon its blindness?

Or was it earth,
Enough to fill a shoe,
And black already
With so much parting
And with so much killing?

Or was it your last road
That brought you a farewell from all the roads
You had walked?

A puddle, a bit of shining metal,
Perhaps the buckle of your enemy's belt,
Or some other small augury
Of heaven?

Oder sandte dir diese Erde,
Die keinen ungeliebt von hinnen gehen lässt
Ein Vogelzeichen durch die Luft,
Erinnernd deine Seele, dass sie zuckte
In ihrem qualverbrannten Leib?

Or did this earth,
Which lets no one depart unloved,
Send you a bird-sign through the air,
Reminding your soul that it quivered
In the torment of its burnt body?

—*Translated by Ruth and Matthew Mead*

Deine Augen, o du mein Geliebter

Ich sah, dass er sah
—JEHUDA ZWI

Deine Augen, o du mein Geliebter,
Waren die Augen der Hindin,
Mit der Pupillen langen Regenbögen
Wie nach fortgezogenen Gottgewittern—
Bienenhaft hatten die Jahrtausende
Den Honig der Gottesnächte darin gesammelt,
Der Sinaifeuer letzte Funken—
O ihr durchsichtigen Türen
Zu den inneren Reichen,
Über denen soviel Wüstensand liegt,
Soviel Qualenmeilen zu o Ihm gehn—
O ihr erloschenen Augen,
Deren Seherkraft nun hinausgefallen ist
In die goldenen Überraschungen des Herrn,
Von denen wir nur die Träume wissen.

Your eyes, O my beloved

I saw that he saw
—JEHUDA ZWI

Your eyes, O my beloved,
Were the eyes of a hind,
With pupils of long rainbows
As when storms of God are gone—
Bee-like the centuries had stored there
The honey of God's nights,
Last sparks of Sinai's fires—
O you transparent doors
To the inner realms,
Over which so much desert sand lies,
So many miles of torment to reach O Him—
O you lifeless eyes
Whose power of prophecy has fallen
Into the golden astonishments of the Lord,
Of which we know only the dreams.

—Translated by Ruth and Matthew Mead

Die Markthändlerin (B.M.)

Sanfte Tiere zu verkaufen war dein Tun auf einem
   Markt auf Erden,
Lockendes sprachst du wie eine Hirtin zu
   den Käuferherden.

Umstrahlt von heimkehrenden Fischen im
   Tränengloriengewand
Versteckten Füssen der Tauben die geschrieben für
   Engel im Sand.

Deine Finger, das blutge Geheimnis berührend
   und abschiedsrot,
Nahmen die kleinen Tode hinein in den riesigen Tod.

The Market Woman (B.M.)

In a market on earth you sold gentle animals,
Spoke temptingly like a shepherdess to buyers
  who flocked round the stalls.

In a gown of tearful glory haloed by fish leaving land
and hidden feet of doves which wrote for angels
  in sand.

Your fingers, touching the bleeding mystery and red
  with parting breath,
Carried the little deaths into enormous death.

   —Translated by Ruth and Matthew Mead

Die Schwachsinnige (B.H.)

Du stiegst auf einen Berg aus Sand
Hilfloses Wandern zu Ihm!
Und glittest hinab; dein Zeichen verschwand.
Für dich stritten die Cherubim.

The Imbecile (B.H.)

You climbed a hill, a sandy one,
A helpless wandering to Him!
Then you slid down; your sign was gone.
For you fought the cherubim.

—*Translated by Ruth and Matthew Mead*

Der Ruhelose (K.F.)

Alle Landstrassen wurden enger und enger.
Wer war dein Bedränger?

Du kamst nie zum Ziel!
Wie im Ziehharmonikaspiel

Wurden sie wieder auseinandergerissen—
Denn auch im Auge ist kein Wissen.

In die blaue Ferne gehn
Berge und Sterne und Apfelbaumalleen.

Windmühlen schlagen wie Stundenuhren
Die Zeit; bis sie verlöscht die Spuren.

The Restless Man (K.F.)

Narrower and narrower grew each avenue
Who was it harassed you?

You went on and on!
Like a full-stretched accordion

The closing roads were torn apart again-
The eye does not know how to attain

The blue distance it sees.
Hills and stars, roads with apple trees.

Like clocks striking the hour windmills strike
Until time erases all the tracks alike.

—Translated by Ruth and Matthew Mead

Die Abenteurerin (A.N.)

Wohl spieltest du mit nichts als Wasserbällen
Die lautlos an der Luft zerschellen.

Aber das siebenfarbige Licht
Gab jeder sein Gesicht.

Einen Herzschlag nur
Wie Engelflur.

Doch dein letztes Abenteuer—
Still; eine Seele ging aus dem Feuer.

The Adventuress (A.N.)

Although you played with bubbles only
Which burst against air silently.

Yet the seven-colored light which shone
Gave each a face of its own.

Like fields where angels meet
The given heartbeat.

But your last adventure—
Hush; a soul went from the fire.

—Translated by Ruth and Matthew Mead

Die Ertrunkene (A.N.)

Immer suchtest du die Perle, am Tage deiner
  Geburt verloren.
Das Besessne suchtest du, Musik der Nacht in
  den Ohren.

Meerumspülte Seele, Taucherin du, bis zum Grunde.
Fische, die Engel der Tiefe, leuchten im Licht
  deiner Wunde.

The Drowned Girl (A.N.)

You always sought the pearl that was lost on the day
   you saw the light.
You sought what is obsessed, in your ears the music
   of night.

Soul washed by the sea, you diver, touching the sea-
   deep ground.
Fish, angels of the depth, gleam in the light of
   your wound.

—Translated by Ruth and Matthew Mead

Die alles Vergessende (A.R.)

Aber im Alter ist alles ein grosses Verschwimmen.
Die kleinen Dinge fliegen fort wie die Immen.

Alle Worte vergasst du und auch den Gegenstand;
Und reichtest deinem Feind über Rosen and Nesseln
    die Hand.

The Woman Who Forgot Everything (A.R.)

But in old age all drifts in blurred immensities.
The little things fly off and up like bees.

You forgot all the words and forgot the object too;
And reached your enemy a hand where roses and
    nettles grew.

—*Translated by Ruth and Matthew Mead*

Chor der Geretteten

Wir Geretteten,
Aus deren hohlem Gebein der Tod schon seine
    Flöten schnitt,
An deren Sehnen der Tod schon seinen Bogen strich—
Unsere Leiber klagen noch nach
Mit ihrer verstümmelten Musik.
Wir Geretteten,
Immer noch hängen die Schlingen für unsere
    Hälse gedreht
Vor uns in der blauen Luft—
Immer noch füllen sich die Stundenuhren mit unserem
    tropfenden Blut.
Wir Geretteten,
Immer noch essen an uns die Würmer der Angst.
Unser Gestirn ist vergraben im Staub.
Wir Geretteten
Bitten euch:
Zeigt uns langsam eure Sonne.
Führt uns von Stern zu Stern im Schritt.
Lasst uns das Leben leise wieder lernen.

Chorus of the Rescued

We, the rescued,
From whose hollow bones death had begun to
    whittle his flutes,
And on whose sinews he had already stroked his bow—
Our bodies continue to lament
With their mutilated music.
We, the rescued,
The nooses wound for our necks still dangle
before us in the blue air—
Hourglasses still fill with our dripping blood.
We, the rescued,
The worms of fear still feed on us.
Our constellation is buried in dust.
We, the rescued,
Beg you:
Show us your sun, but gradually.
Lead us from star to star, step by step.
Be gentle when you teach us to live again.
Lest the song of a bird,

Es könnte sonst eines Vogels Lied,
Das Füllen des Eimers am Brunnen
Unseren schlecht versiegelten Schmerz
  aufbrechen lassen
Und uns wegschäumen—
Wir bitten euch:
Zeigt uns noch nicht einen beissenden Hund—
Es könnte sein, es könnte sein
Dass wir zu Staub zerfallen—
Vor euren Augen zerfallen in Staub.
Was hält denn unsere Webe zusammen?
Wir odemlos gewordene,
Deren Seele zu Ihm floh aus der Mittemacht
Lange bevor man unseren Leib rettete
In die Arche des Augenblicks.
Wir Geretteten,
Wir drücken eure Hand,
Wir erkennen euer Auge—
Aber zusammen hält uns nur noch der Abschied,
Der Abschied im Staub
Hält uns mit euch zusammen.

Or a pail being filled at the well,
Let our badly sealed pain burst forth again
and carry us away—
We beg you:
Do not show us an angry dog, not yet—
It could be, it could be
That we will dissolve into dust—
Dissolve into dust before your eyes.
For what binds our fabric together?
We whose breath vacated us,
Whose soul fled to Him out of that midnight
Long before our bodies were rescued
Into the ark of the moment.
We, the rescued,
We press your hand
We look into your eye—
But all that binds us together now is leave-taking
The leave-taking in the dust
Binds us together with you.

—Translated by Michael Roloff

Chor der Wandernden

Wir Wandernde,
Unsere Wege ziehen wir als Gepäck hinter uns her—
Mit einem Fetzen des Landes darin wir Rast hielten
Sind wir bekleidet—
Aus dem Kochtopf der Sprache, die wir unter
    Tränen erlernten,
Ernähren wir uns.

Wir Wandernde,
An jeder Wegkreuzung erwartet uns eine Tür
Dahinter das Reh, der waisenäugige Israel der Tiere
In seine rauschenden Wälder verschwindet
Und die Lerche über den goldenen Äckern jauchzt.
Ein Meer von Einsamkeit steht mit uns still
Wo wir anklopfen.
O ihr Hüter mit flammenden Schwertern ausgerüstet,
Die Staubkörner unter unseren Wanderfüssen
Beginnen schon das Blut in unseren Enkeln
    zu treiben—
O wir Wandernde vor den Türen der Erde,
Vom Grüssen in die Ferne

Chorus of the Wanderers

We, the wanderers,
We drag the ways we have come like burdens
 behind us—
We are clad in the rags of the land
In which we rested—
We feed ourselves from the cooking pot of the language
That we learned with tears.

We, the wanderers,
At every crossroad a door awaits us
Behind which the roe, the orphan-eyed Israel
 of animals
Vanishes into its murmuring forests
And the lark exults above the golden fields.
A sea of loneliness stands silently beside us
Where we knock.
O you guardians armed with flaming swords,
The grains of dust beneath our wandering feet
Have begun to stir our grandsons' blood—
O we wanderers before the doors of earth,
From saluting into the distance

Haben unsere Hüte schon Sterne angesteckt.
Wie Zollstöcke liegen unsere Leiber auf der Erde
Und messen den Horizont aus—

O wir Wandernde,
Kriechende Würmer für kommende Schuhe,
Unser Tod wird wie eine Schwelle liegen
Vor euren verschlossenen Türen!

Our hats have lit up stars.
Like measuring rods our bodies lie on the earth
And measure out the horizon—

O we, the wanderers,
Crawling worms for coming shoes,
Our death will lie like a threshold
Before your tight-shut doors!

—Translated by Ruth and Matthew Mead

Chor der Waisen

Wir Waisen
Wir klagen der Welt:
Herabgehauen hat man unseren Ast
Und ins Feuer geworfen—
Brennholz hat man aus unseren Beschützern
   gemacht—
Wir Waisen liegen auf den Feldern der Einsamkeit.
Wir Waisen
Wir klagen der Welt:
In der Nacht spielen unsere Eltern Verstecken
   mit uns—
Hinter den schwarzen Falten der Nacht
Schauen uns ihre Gesichter an,
Sprechen ihre Münder:
Dürrholz waren wir in eines Holzhauers Hand—
Aber unsere Augen sind Engelaugen geworden
Und sehen euch an,
Durch die schwarzen Falten der Nacht
Blicken sie hindurch—

Chorus of the Orphans

We orphans
We lament to the world:
Our branch has been cut down
And thrown in the fire—
Kindling was made of our protectors—
We orphans lie stretched out on the fields
    of loneliness.
We orphans
We lament to the world:
At night our parents play hide and seek—
From behind the black folds of night
Their faces gaze at us,
Their mouths speak:
Kindling we were in a woodcutter's hand—
But our eyes have become angel eyes
And regard you,
Through the black folds of night
They penetrate—

Wir Waisen
Wir klagen der Welt:
Steine sind unser Spielzeug geworden,
Steine haben Gesichter, Vater- und Muttergesichter
Sie verwelken nicht wie Blumen, sie beissen nicht
   wie Tiere—
Und sie brennen nicht wie Dürrholz, wenn man sie
   in den Ofen wirft—
Wir Waisen wir klagen der Welt:
Welt warum hast du uns die weichen
   Mütter genommen
Und die Väter, die sagen: Mein Kind du gleichst mir!
Wir Waisen gleichen niemand mehr auf der Welt!
O Welt
Wir klagen dich an!

We orphans
We lament to the world:
Stones have become our playthings,
Stones have faces, father and mother faces
They wilt not like flowers, nor bite like beasts—
And burn not like tinder when tossed into the oven—
We orphans we lament to the world:
World, why have you taken our soft mothers from us
And the fathers who say: My child, you are like me!
We orphans are like no one in this world any more!
O world
We accuse you!

—Translated by Michael Roloff

Chor der Toten

Wir von der schwarzen Sonne der Angst
Wie Siebe Zerstochenen—
Abgeronnene sind wir vom Schweiss
   der Todesminute.
Abgewelkt an unserem Leibe sind die uns
   angetanen Tode
Wie Feldblumen abgewelkt an einem Hügel Sand.
O ihr, die ihr noch den Staub grüsst als einen Freund
Die ihr, redender Sand zum Sande sprecht:
Ich liebe dich.

Wir sagen euch:
Zerrissen sind die Mäntel der Staubgeheimnisse
Die Lüfte, die man in uns erstickte,
Die Feuer, darin man uns brannte,
Die Erde, darin man unseren Abhub warf.
Das Wasser, das mit unserem Angstschweiss
   dahinperlte
Ist mit uns aufgebrochen und beginnt zu glänzen.
Wir Toten Israels sagen euch:
Wir reichen schon einen Stern weiter
In unseren verborgenen Gott hinein.

Chorus of the Dead

We from the black sun of fear
Holed like sieves—
We dripped from the sweat of death's minute.
Withered on our bodies are the deaths done unto us
Like flowers of the field withered on a hill of sand.
O you who still greet the dust as friend
You who talking sand say to the sand:
I love you.

We say to you:
Torn are the cloaks of the mysteries of dust
The air in which we were suffocated,
The fires in which we were burned,
The earth into which our remains were cast.
The water which was beaded with our sweat of fear
Has broken forth with us and begins to gleam.
We dead of Israel say to you:
We are moving past one more star
Into our hidden God.

—*Translated by Ruth and Matthew Mead*

Chor der Schatten

Wir Schatten, o wir Schatten!
Schatten von Henkern
Geheftet am Staube eurer Untaten—
Schatten von Opfern
Zeichnend das Drama eures Blutes an eine Wand.
O wir hilflosen Trauerfalter
Eingefangen auf einem Stern, der ruhig weiterbrennt
Wenn wir in Höllen tanzen müssen.
Unsere Marionettenspieler wissen nur noch den Tod.

Goldene Amme, die du uns nährst
Zu solcher Verzweiflung,
Wende ab o Sonne dein Angesicht
Auf dass auch wir versinken—
Oder lass uns spiegeln eines Kindes jauchzend
Erhobene Finger
Und einer Libelle leichtes Glück
Uber dem Brunnenrand.

Chorus of the Shadows

We shadows, O we shadows!
Shadows of hangmen
Pinned to the dust of your crimes—
Shadows of victims
Silhouetting the drama of your blood on a wall.
O we helpless moths of mourning
Caught in a star that calmly goes on burning
When we must dance in hell.
Our puppeteers know nothing but death any more.

Golden nurse, you who feed us
For such despair,
Turn away, O sun, your countenance
So that we too may sink away—
Or let us mirror a child's
Fingers raised in joy
And a dragonfly's flimsy luck
Above the rim of a well.

  —Translated by Michael Roloff

Chor der Steine

Wir Steine
Wenn einer uns hebt
Hebt er Urzeiten empor—
Wenn einer uns hebt
Hebt er den Garten Eden empor—
Wenn einer uns hebt
Hebt er Adam und Evas Erkenntnis empor
Und der Schlange staubessende Verführung.

Wenn einer uns hebt
Hebt er Billionen Erinnerungen in seiner Hand
Die sich nicht auflösen im Blute
Wie der Abend.
Denn Gedenksteine sind wir
Alles Sterben umfassend.

Chorus of the Stones

We stones
When someone lifts us
He lifts the Foretime—
When someone lifts us
He lifts the Garden of Eden—
When someone lifts us
He lifts the knowledge of Adam and Eve
And the serpent's dust-eating seduction.

When someone lifts us
He lifts in his hand millions of memories
Which do not dissolve in blood
Like evening.
For we are memorial stones
Embracing all dying.

Ein Ranzen voll gelebten Lebens sind wir.
Wer uns hebt, hebt die hartgewordenen
    Gräber der Erde.
Ihr Jakobshäupter,
Die Wurzeln der Träume halten wir versteckt für euch,
Lassen die luftigen Engelsleitern
Wie Ranken eines Windenbeetes spriessen.

Wenn einer ims anrührt
Rührt er eine Klagemauer an.
Wie der Diamant zerschneidet eure Klage unsere Härte
Bis sie zerfällt und weiches Herz wird—
Während ihr versteint.
Wenn einer uns anrührt
Rührt er die Wegscheiden der Mittemacht an
Klingend von Geburt und Tod.

Wenn einer uns wirft—
Wirft er den Garten Eden—
Den Wein der Sterne—
Die Augen der Liebenden und alien Verrat—

We are a satchel full of lived life.
Whoever lifts us lifts the hardened graves of earth.
You heads of Jacob,
For you we hide the roots of dreams
And let the airy angels' ladders
Sprout like the tendrils of a bed of bindweed.

When someone touches us
He touches the wailing wall.
Like a diamond your lament cuts our hardness
Until it crumbles and becomes a soft heart—
While you turn to stone.
When someone touches us
He touches the forked ways of midnight
Sounding with birth and death.

When someone throws us—
He throws the Garden of Eden—
The wine of the stars—
The eyes of the lovers and all betrayal—

Wenn einer uns wirft im Zorne
So wirft er Äonen gebrochener Herzen
Und seidener Schmetterlinge.

Hütet euch, hütet euch
Zu werfen im Zorne mit einem Stein—
Unser Gemisch ist ein vom Odem Durchblasenes.
Es erstarrte im Geheimnis
Aber kann erwachen an einem Kuss.

When someone throws us in anger
He throws aeons of broken hearts
And silken butterflies.

Beware, beware
Of throwing a stone in anger—
Breath once transfused our minglement,
Which grew solid in secret
But can awaken at a kiss.

—Translated by Ruth and Matthew Mead

Chor der Sterne

Wir Sterne, wir Sterne
Wir wandernder, glänzender, singender Staub—
Unsere Schwester die Erde ist die Blinde geworden
Unter den Leuchtbildern des Himmels—
Ein Schrei ist sie geworden
Unter den Singenden—
Sie, die Sehnsuchtsvollste
Die im Staube begann ihr Werk: Engel zu bilden—
Sie, die die Seligkeit in ihrem Geheimnis trägt
Wie goldführendes Gewässer—
Ausgeschüttet in der Nacht liegt sie
Wie Wein auf den Gassen—
Des Bösen gelbe Schwefellichter hüpfen auf
    ihrem Leib.

O Erde, Erde
Stern aller Sterne
Durchzogen von den Spuren des Heimwehs
Die Gott selbst begann—
Ist niemand auf dir, der sich erinnert an deine Jugend?

Chorus of the Stars

We stars, we stars
We wandering, glistening, singing dust—
Earth, our sister, has gone blind
Among the constellations of heaven—
A scream she has become
Among the singers—
She, richest in longing
Who began her task—to form angels—in dust,
She whose secret contains bliss
Like streams bearing gold—
Poured out into the night she lies
Like wine in the streets—
Evil's yellow sulfur lights flicker over her body.

O earth, earth
Star of stars
Veined by the spoors of homesickness
Begun by God Himself—
Have you no one who remembers your youth?

Niemand, der sich hingibt als Schwimmer
Den Meeren von Tod?
Ist niemandes Sehnsucht reif geworden
Dass sie sich erhebt wie der engelhaft fliegende Samen
Der Löwenzahnblüte?

Erde, Erde, bist du eine Blinde geworden
Vor den Schwesternaugen der Plejaden
Oder der Waage prüfendem Blick?

Mörderhände gaben Israel einen Spiegel
Darin es sterbend sein Sterben erblickte—

Erde, o Erde
Stern aller Sterne
Einmal wird ein Sternbild Spiegel heissen.
Dann o Blinde wirst du wieder sehn!

No one who will surrender himself as the swimmer
To the oceans of death?
Has no one's longing ripened
So it will rise like the angelically flying seed
Of the dandelion blossom?

Earth, earth, have you gone blind
Before the sister eyes of the Pleiades
Or Libra's examining gaze?

Murder hands gave Israel a mirror
In which it recognized its death while dying—

Earth, O earth
Star of stars
One day a constellation will be called *mirror.*
Then, O blind one, you will see again!

—Translated by Michael Roloff

Chor der unsichtbaren Dinge

Klagemauer Nacht!
Eingegraben in dir sind die Psalmen des Schweigens.
Die Fusspuren, die sich fullten mit Tod
Wie reifende Äpfel
Haben bei dir nach Hause gefunden.
Die Tränen, die dein schwarzes Moos feuchten
Werden schon eingesammelt.

Denn der Engel mit den Körben
Für die unsichtbaren Dinge ist gekommen.
O die Blicke der auseinandergerissenen Liebenden
Die Himmelschaffenden, die Weltengebärenden
Wie werden sie sanft für die Ewigkeit gepflückt
Und gedeckt mit dem Schlaf des gemordeten Kindes,
In dessen warmem Dunkel
Die Sehnsüchte neuer Herrlichkeiten keimen.

Im Geheimnis eines Seufzers
Kann das ungesungene Lied des Friedens keimen.

Chorus of Invisible Things

Wailing-wall night!
Engraved on you are the psalms of silence.
The footprints, which filled with death
Like ripening apples,
Have found their way home to you.
The tears which moisten your black moss
Are being collected.

Because the angel with the baskets
For invisible things has come.
O the glances of the lovers torn apart
The heaven-creating, the world-bearing
How softly they are plucked for eternity
And covered with the sleep of the murdered child,
In whose warm dark
The longings of new glories germinate.

In the secret of a sigh
The unsung song of peace can germinate.

Klagemauer Nacht,
Von dem Blitze eines Gebetes kannst du
  zer trümmert werden
Und alle, die Gott verschlafen haben
Wachen hinter deinen stürzenden Mauern
Zu ihm auf.

Wailing-wall night,
You can be smashed by the lightning of a prayer
And all who overslept God
Will wake to him
Behind your falling wall.

 —*Translated by Ruth and Matthew Mead*

Chor der Wolken

Wir sind voller Seufzer, voller Blicke
Wir sind voller Lachen
Und zuweilen tragen wir eure Gesichter.
Wir sind euch nicht fern.
Wer weiss, wieviel von eurem Blute aufstieg
Und uns färbte?
Wer weiss, wieviel Tränen ihr durch unser Weinen
Vergossen habt? Wieviel Sehnsucht uns formte?
Sterbespieler sind wir
Gewöhnen euch sanft an den Tod.
Ihr Ungeübten, die in den Nächten nichts lernen.
Viele Engel sind euch gegeben
Aber ihr seht sie nicht.

Chorus of Clouds

We are full of sighs, full of glances,
We are full of laughter
And sometimes we wear your faces.
We are not far from you.
Who knows how much of your blood rose
And stained us?
Who knows how many tears you have shed
Because of our weeping? How much longing
    formed us?
We play at dying,
Accustom you gently to death.
You, the inexperienced, who learn nothing in the nights.
Many angels are given you
But you do not see them.

—Translated by Ruth and Matthew Mead

Chor der Bäume

O ihr Gejagten alle auf der Welt!
Unsere Sprache ist gemischt aus Quellen und Sternen
Wie die eure.
Eure Buchstaben sind aus unserem Fleisch.
Wir sind die steigend Wandernden
Wir erkennen euch—
O ihr Gejagten auf der Welt!
Heute hing die Hindin Mensch an unseren Zweigen
Gestern färbte das Reh die Weide mit Rosen urn
    unseren Stamm.
Eurer Fusspuren letzte Angst löscht aus in unserem
    Frieden
Wir sind der grosse Schattenzeiger
Den Vogelsang umspielt—
O ihr Gejagten alle auf der Welt!
Wir zeigen in ein Geheimnis
Das mit der Nacht beginnt.

Chorus of Trees

O all you hunted of the world!
Our speech is mixed from springs and stars
Like yours.
Your letters are of our flesh.
We are the climbing wanderers
We recognize you—
O you hunted of the world!
Today the man like a hind hung on our branches
Yesterday the deer stained the meadows around our
    trunks with roses
The last fear of your footprints is extinguished in
    our peace,
We are the great shadow-pointer
Played round by birdsong—
O all you hunted of the world!
We point into a secret
Which begins with night.

—Translated by Ruth and Matthew Mead

Chor der Tröster

Gärtner sind wir, blumenlos gewordene
Kein Heilkraut lässt sich pflanzen
Von Gestern nach Morgen.
Der Salbei hat abgeblüht in den Wiegen—
Rosmarin seinen Duft im Angesicht der neuen
   Toten verloren—
Selbst der Wermut war bitter nur für gestern.
Die Blüten des Trostes sind zu kurz entsprossen
Reichen nicht für die Qual einer Kinderträne.

Neuer Same wird vielleicht
Im Herzen ernes nächtlichen Sängers gezogen.
Wer von uns darf trösten?
In der Tiefe des Hohlwegs
Zwischen Gestern und Morgen
Steht der Cherub
Mahlt mit seinen Flügeln die Blitze der Trauer
Seine Hände aber halten die Felsen auseinander
Von Gestern und Morgen
Wie die Ränder einer Wunde

Chorus of Comforters

We are gardeners who have no flowers.
No herb may be transplanted
From yesterday to tomorrow.
The sage has faded in the cradles—
Rosemary lost its scent facing the new dead—
Even wormwood was only bitter yesterday.
The blossoms of comfort are too small
Not enough for the torment of a child's tear.

New seed may perhaps be gathered
In the heart of a nocturnal singer.
Which of us may comfort?
In the depth of the defile
Between yesterday and tomorrow
The cherub stands
Grinding the lightnings of sorrow with his wings
But his hands hold apart the rocks
Of yesterday and tomorrow
Like the edges of a wound

Die offenbleiben soll
Die noch nicht heilen darf.

Nicht einschlafen lassen die Blitze der Trauer
Das Feld des Vergessens.

Wer von uns darf trösten?

Gärtner sind wir, blumenlos gewordene
Und stehn auf einem Stern, der strahlt
Und weinen.

Which must remain open
That may not yet heal.

The lightnings of sorrow do not allow
The field of forgetting to fall asleep.

Which of us may comfort?

We are gardeners who have no flowers
And stand upon a shining star
And weep.

 —*Translated by Ruth and Matthew Mead*

Chor der Ungeborenen

Wir Ungeborenen
Schon beginnt die Sehnsucht an uns zu schaffen
Die Ufer des Blutes weiten sich zu unserem Empfang
Wie Tau sinken wir in die Liebe hinein.
Noch liegen die Schatten der Zeit wie Fragen
Über unserem Geheimnis.

Ihr Liebenden,
Ihr Sehnsüchtigen,
Hört, ihr Abschiedskranken:
Wir sind es, die in euren Blicken zu leben beginnen,
In euren Händen, die suchende sind in der
    blauen Luft—
Wir sind es, die nach Morgen Duftenden.
Schon zieht uns euer Atem ein,
Nimmt uns hinab in euren Schlaf
In die Träume, die unser Erdreich sind
Wo unsere schwarze Amme, die Nacht

Chorus of the Unborn

We the unborn
The yearning has begun to plague us
The shores of blood broaden to receive us
Like dew we sink into love
But still the shadows of time lie like questions
Over our secret.

You who love,
You who yearn,
Listen, you who are sick with parting:
We are those who begin to live in your glances,
In your hands which are searching the blue air—
We are those who smell of morning.
Already your breath is inhaling us,
Drawing us down into your sleep
Into the dreams which are our earth
Where night, our black nurse,

Uns wachsen lässt,
Bis wir uns spiegeln in euren Augen
Bis wir sprechen in euer Ohr.

Schmetterlmgsgleich
Werden wir von den Häschern eurer
    Sehnsucht gefangen—
Wie Vogelstimmen an die Erde verkauft—
Wir Morgenduftenden,
Wir kommenden Lichter für eure Traurigkeit.

Lets us grow
Until we mirror ourselves in your eyes
Until we speak into your ear.

We are caught
Like butterflies by the sentries of your yearning—
Like birdsong sold to earth—
We who smell of morning,
We future lights for your sorrow.

　　—Translated by Ruth and Matthew Mead

Stimme des Heiligen Landes

O meine Kinder,
Der Tod ist durch eure Herzen gefahren
Wie durch einen Weinberg—
Malte *Israel* rot an alle Wände der Erde.

Wo soll die kleine Heiligkeit hin
Die noch in meinem Sande wohnt?
Durch die Röhren der Abgeschiedenheit
Sprechen die Stimmen der Toten:

Leget auf den Acker die Waffen der Rache
Damit sie leise werden—
Denn auch Eisen und Korn sind Geschwister
Im Schosse der Erde—

Wo soll denn die kleine Heiligkeit hin
Die noch in meinem Sande wohnt?

The voice of the Holy Land

O my children,
Death has run through your hearts
As through a vineyard—
Painted *Israel* red on all the walls of the world.

What shall be the end of the little holiness
Which still dwells in my sand?
The voices of the dead
Speak through reed pipes of seclusion.

Lay the weapons of revenge in the field
That they grow gentle—
For even iron and grain are akin
In the womb of earth—

But what shall be the end of the little holiness
Which still dwells in my sand?

Das Kind im Schlafe gemordet
Steht auf; biegt den Baum der Jahrtausende hinab
Und heftet den weissen, atmenden Stern
Der einmal Israel hiess
An seine Krone.
Schnelle zurück, spricht es
Dorthin, wo Tränen Ewigkeit bedeuten.

The child murdered in sleep
Arises; bends down the tree of ages
And pins the white breathing star
That was once called Israel
To its topmost bough.
Spring upright again, says the child,
To where tears mean eternity.

—Translated by Ruth and Matthew Mead

Sternverdunkelung (1949)

Eclipse of the Stars

in memory of my father

Wenn wie Raunch der Schlaf einzieht in
den Leib

Wenn wie Rauch der Schlaf einzieht in den Leib,
und wie ein erloschenes Gestirn, das anderswo
    entzündet wird,
der Mensch zu Grunde fährt,
steht der Streit still,
abgetriebene Mähre, die den Albdruck ihres Reiters
abgeworfen hat.
Aus ihrem heimlichen Takt entlassen
sind die Schritte,
die wie Brunnenschwengel an das Rätsel der
    Erde klopften
Alle künstlichen Tode sind in ihre blutverwirrten
    Nester heimgekehrt.

Wenn wie Rauch der Schlaf einzieht in den Leib,
atmet das Kind gestillt, mit der Mondtrompete im Arm.
Die Träne verschläft ihre Sehnsucht zu fliessen,
aber die Liebe ist alle Umwege zu Ende gegangen
und ruht in ihrem Beginn.

When sleep enters the body
like smoke

When sleep enters the body like smoke
and man journeys into the abyss
like an extinguished star that is lighted elsewhere,
then all quarrel ceases,
overworked nag that has tossed the nightmare grip
of its rider.
Released from their secret rhythm
are the steps
that knock like well lifts at the earth's enigma.
All artificial deaths have returned to the bloody
    confusion of their nests.

When sleep enters the body like smoke
the stilled child breathes with the moon trumpet in
    its arm.
The tear oversleeps its longing to flow,
but love has completed all detours
and rests in its beginning.

Jetzt ist die Zeit für das Kalb seine neue Zunge
am Leib der Mutter zu proben,
der falsche Schlüssel schliesst nicht
und das Messer rostet hinein
bis in die blasse Heide der Morgendämmerung
die aus der Vergessenheit erblüht im
     furchtbaren Frührot.

Wenn wie Rauch der Schlaf auszieht aus dem Leib,
und der Mensch geheimnisgesättigt
die abgetriebene Mähre des Streites
aus dem Stalle treibt,
beginnt die feuerschnaubende Verbindung aufs neue
und der Tod enwacht in jeder Maienknospe
und das Kind küsst einen Stein
in der Sternverdunkelung.

Now is the time for the calf to test
its new tongue on its mother's body,
the wrong key does not lock
and the knife rusts far
into the pale heath of dawn
which blossoms out of the oblivion
with the early morning's fearful red.

When sleep leaves the body like smoke
and man, sated with secrets,
drives the overworked nag of quarrel
out of its stall,
then the fire-breathing union begins anew
and death wakens in every bud of May
and the child kisses a stone
in the eclipse of the stars.

   —Translated by Michael Roloff

Engel der Bittenden

Engel der Bittenden,
nun, wo das Feuer wie ein reissendes Abendrot
alles Bewohnte verbrannte zu Nacht—
Mauern und Geräte, den Herd und die Wiege,
die alle abgefallenes Stückgut der Sehnsucht sind—
Sehnsucht, die fliegt im blauen Segel der Luft!

Engel der Bittenden,
auf des Todes weissem Boden, der nichts mehr trägt,
wächst der in Verzweiflung gepflanzte Wald.
Wald aus Armen mit der Hände Gezweig,
eingekrallt in die Feste der Nacht, in
    den Sternenmantel.
Oder den Tod pflügend, ihn, der das Leben bewahrt.

Engel der Bittenden,
im Wald, der nicht rauscht,
wo die Schatten Totenmaler sind
und die durchsichtigen Tränen der Liebenden
das Samenkorn.

Angel of supplicants

Angel of supplicants,
now, when the fire like a raging sunset
has burned down into night everything inhabited—
walls and implements, the stove and the cradle,
which are all jettisoned part-loads of longing—
longing, which flies in the blue sail of the air!

Angel of supplicants,
on the white floor of death, which supports
   nothing now,
grows the forest planted in despair.
Forest of arms with hands for branches,
clawed into the fortress of night, into the cloak of stars.
Or plowing death, death which preserves life.

Angel of supplicants,
in the forest, that does not roar,
where shadows are painters of death
and transparent tears of lovers
the seed.

Wie vom Sturm ergriffen, reissen
die mondverhafteten Mütter ihre Wurzeln aus
und mit Knistern der Greise Dürrholz verfällt.
Aber immer noch spielen die Kinder im Sande,
formen übend ein Neues aus der Nacht heraus
denn warm sind sie noch von der Verwandlung.

Engel der Bittenden,
segne den Sand,
lass ihn die Sprache der Sehnsucht verstehn,
daraus ein Neues wachsen will aus Kinderhand,
immer ein Neues!

As if gripped by storm,
the moon-habituated mothers tear out their roots
and dry wood crumbles with an old man's crackle.
But the children are still playing in the sand,
forming, as they practice, something new out of night
for they are still warm from the metamorphosis.

Angel of supplicants,
bless the sand,
let it understand the language of longing,
from which something new wants to grow out of the
    hands of children,
always something new!

—*Translated by Ruth and Matthew Mead*

Nacht, Nacht

Nacht, Nacht,
dass du nicht in Scherben zerspringst,
nun wo die Zeit mit den reissenden Sonnen
des Martyriums
in deiner meergedeckten Tiefe untergeht—
die Monde des Todes
das stürzende Erdendach
in deines Schweigens geronnenes Blut ziehn—

Nacht, Nacht,
einmal warst du der Geheimnisse Braut
schattenliliengeschmückt—
In deinem dunklen Glase glitzerte
die Fata Morgana der Sehnsüchtigen
und die Liebe hatte ihre Morgenrose
dir zum Erblühen hingestellt—
Einmal warst du der Traummalereien
jenseitiger Spiegel und orakelnder Mund—

Night, Night

Night, night,
that you may not shatter in fragments
now when time sinks with the ravenous suns
of martyrdom
in your sea-covered depths—
the moons of death
drag the falling roof of earth
into the congealed blood of your silence.

Night, night,
once you were the bride of mysteries
adorned with lilies of shadow—
In your dark glass sparkled
the mirage of all who yearn
and love had set its morning rose
to blossom before you—
You were once the oracular mouth
of dream painting and mirrored the beyond.

Nacht, Nacht,
jetzt bist du der Friedhof
für eines Sternes schrecklichen Schiffbruch
    geworden—
sprachlos taucht die Zeit in dir unter
mit ihrem Zeichen:
Der stürzende Stein
und die Fahne aus Rauch!

Night, night,
now you are the graveyard
for the terrible shipwreck of a star—
time sinks speechless in you
with its sign:
The falling stone
and the flag of smoke.

—*Translated by Ruth and Matthew Mead*

Auf daß die Verfolgten nicht
Verfolger werden

Schritte—
In welchen Grotten der Echos
seid ihr bewahrt,
die ihr den Ohren einst weissagtet
kommenden Tod?

Schritte—
Nicht Vogelflug, noch Schau der Eingeweide,
noch der blutschwitzende Mars
gab des Orakels Todesauskunft mehr—
nur Schritte—

Schritte—
Urzeitspiel von Henker und Opfer,
Verfolger und Verfolgten,
Jäger und Gejagt—

That the persecuted may not become persecutors

Footsteps—
In which of Echo's grottoes
are you preserved,
you who once prophesied aloud
the coming of death?

Footsteps—
Neither bird-flight, inspection of entrails,
nor Mars sweating blood
confirmed the oracle's message of death—
only footsteps—

Footsteps—
Age-old game of hangman and victim,
Persecutor and persecuted,
Hunter and hunted—

Schritte
die die Zeit reissend machen
die Stunde mit Wölfen behängen,
dem Flüchtling die Flucht auslöschen
im Blute.

Schritte
die Zeit zählend mit Schreien, Seufzern,
Austritt des Blutes bis es gerinnt,
Todesschweiss zu Stunden häufend—

Schritte der Henker
über Schritten der Opfer,
Sekundenzeiger im Gang der Erde,
von welchem Schwarzmond schrecklich gezogen?

In der Musik der Sphären
wo schrillt euer Ton?

Footsteps
which turn time ravenous
emblazoning the hour with wolves
extinguishing the flight in the fugitive's
blood.

Footsteps
measuring time with screams, groans,
the seeping of blood until it congeals,
heaping up hours of sweaty death—

Steps of hangmen
over the steps of victims,
what black moon pulled with such terror
the sweep-hand in earth's orbit?

Where does your note shrill
in the music of the spheres?

   —Translated by Ruth and Matthew Mead

O du weinendes Herz der Welt!

O du weinendes Herz der Welt!
Zwiespältig Samenkorn
aus Leben und Tod.
Von dir wollte Gott gefunden werden
Keimblatt der Liebe.

Bist du verborgen in einer Waise,
die am Geländer des Lebens
schwer sich stützend weitergeht?
Wohnst du bei ihr, dort
wo der Stern sein sicherstes Versteck hat?

O du weinendes Herz der Welt!
Auch du wirst auffahren
wenn die Zeit erfüllt ist.
Denn nicht häuslich darf die Sehnsucht bleiben
die brückenbauende
von Stern zu Stern!

O you weeping heart of the world!

O you weeping heart of the world!
Twofold seed
made of life and death.
God wanted to be found by you
seed-leaf of love.

Are you hidden in an orphan girl
who walks on, leaning heavily
on the railing of life?
Do you dwell with her, there
where the star has its safest hiding place?

O you weeping heart of the world!
You too will ascend
when time is fulfilled.
For the longing
that builds bridges
from star to star
must not remain domestic!

—*Translated by Ruth and Matthew Mead*

Erde

Erde,
alle Saiten deines Todes haben sie angezogen,
zu Ende haben sie deinen Sand geküsst;
der 1st schwarz geworden
von soviel Abschied und soviel Tod bereiten.

Oder fühlen sie, dass du sterben musst?
Die Sonne ihr Lieblingskind verlieren wird
und deine Ozeane,
deine schäumenden, lichtentzündeten Wasserpferde
an den Mond geseilt werden,
der in azurgefärbter Nacht
ein neues Becken für die Sehnsucht weiss?

Erde,
viele Wunden schlagen sie in deme Rinde
deine Sternenschrift zu lesen
die in Nächte gehüllt ist bis zu Seinem Thron hinauf.

Earth

Earth,
they have tightened all the strings of your death,
they have kissed to the last your sand
which has grown black
with preparing so much parting and so much death.

Or do they feel that you must die?
That the sun will lose its favorite child
and that your oceans,
your foaming, light-fired steeds of sea
will be harnessed to the moon
which in azure-colored night
will know a new vessel for longing?

Earth,
they strike many wounds into your crust
to read your starry script
which is cloaked in nights up to His very throne.

Aber wie Pilze wachsen die kleinen Tode
an ihren Händen,
damit löschen sie deine Leuchten,
schliessen die Wächteraugen der Cherubim
und die Engel, die Tränenverspäteten, die Goldgräber
in den Schmerzgebirgen,
die Blumen aus dem Blätterwerk Mensch,
haben sie wieder tief unter den Grabsteinen
der Tiergötter vergraben.

Erde,
wenn auch ihre Liebe ausgewandert ist,
ihre Brände ausgebrannt,
und es leise geworden ist auf dir und leer—

vielleicht augenlose Stelle am Himmel,
darin andere Gestirne zu leuchten beginnen
bienenhaft vom Dufte des Gewesenen angezogen—

so wird dein namenloser Staub, den sie benannt,
dem sie soviele Wandernamen gaben
durch sie ins Gold der Ewigkeit gemünzt
doch seine selige Heimat haben.

But the little deaths grow like fungus
on their hands
with which they quench your lights,
and close the guardian eyes of the cherubim
and they have again buried the angels, the
     late lamenters,
the diggers for gold in the mountains of pain,
the flowers of the foliage of man,
deep under the gravestones
of the animal gods.

Earth,
even if their love has gone into exile,
though their conflagrations are burnt out,
and it has grown quiet upon you and empty—

perhaps an eyeless place in the sky
in which other constellations begin to shine
drawn like bees by the scent of what has been—

so your nameless dust, which they named,
to which they gave so many nomad names
will be minted by them into the gold of eternity
but still have its blessed home.

  —*Translated by Ruth and Matthew Mead*

O ihr Tiere!

O ihr Tiere!

Euer Schicksal dreht sich wie der Sekundenzeiger
mit kleinen Schritten
in der Menschheit unerlösten Stunde.

Und nur der Hahnenschrei,
mondaufgezogen,
weiss vielleicht
eure uralte Zeit!

Wie mit Steinen zugedeckt ist uns
eure reissende Sehnsucht
und wissen nicht was brüllt
im abschiedrauchenden Stall,
wenn das Kalb von der Mutter
gerissen wird.

Was schweigt im Element des Leidens
der Fisch zappelnd zwischen Wasser und Land?

O you animals!

O you animals!

Your fate turns like the second-hand
with small steps
in the unredeemed hour of mankind.

And only the cockcrow,
wound up by the moon,
knows perhaps
your ancient time!

As if covered with stones
is your violent longing to us
and we do not know what bellows
in the smoking stable of parting
when the calf is torn
from its mother.

How does the fish, struggling between water and land,
keep silent in the element of suffering?

Wieviel kriechender und geflügelter Staub
an unseren Schuhsohlen,
die stehn wie offene Gräber am Abend?

O der kriegszerrissene Leib des Pferdes
an dem fraglos die Fliegen stechen
und die Ackerblume durch die leere Augenhöhle
    wächst!

Nicht der sterndeutende Bileam
wusste von eurem Geheimnis,
als seine Eselin
den Engel im Auge behielt!

How much creeping and winged dust
on the soles of our shoes,
which stand like open graves at evening?

Oh, the horse's war-torn body
where flies without question sting
and the wildflower grows through the empty
    eye socket!

Not even Balaam, prophet of the star,
knew of your secret
as his ass
beheld the angel!

—*Translated by Ruth and Matthew Mead*

Golem Tod!

Golem Tod!
Ein Gerüst ist gestellt
und die Zimmerleute gekommen
und wie die Meute der Hunde
lechzend,
laufen sie deiner Schattenspirale nach.

Golem Tod!
Nabel der Welt,
dein Skelett breitet die Arme
mit falschem Segen!
Deine Rippen legen sich auf die Breitengrade
   der Erde
richtig zugemessen!

Golem Tod!
Am Bette des Waisenkindes
stehen die vier Cherubim
mit vorgeschlagenen Flügeln,
angesichtsverhüllt—

Golem death!

Golem death!
A scaffold is prepared
and the carpenters are come
and like a pack of hounds
slavering,
they track your shadow-spiral.

Golem death!
Navel of the world,
your skeleton spreads its arms
in false blessing!
You lay your ribs along earth's latitudes
fitting exactly!

Golem death!
Four cherubim stand
by the bed of the orphan child
wings folded forward
hiding their faces—

während auf den Feldern
das Kraut der Entzweiung gepflanzt wird
und verfallene Gärtner
am Mond die Äpfel reifen lassen!

Am Sternenhimmel aber wiegt
der Greis mit der Waage
das weinende Ende
von der Wolke zum Wurm!

Golem Tod!
Niemand aber vermag dich zu heben
aus der Zeit hinaus—
denn geborgt ist dein Rauschblut
und dein eisenumschütteter Leib
zerfällt mit allem Kehricht
wieder in den Beginn!

In den Ruinen aber wohnt doppelte Sehnsucht!
Der Stein umschläft grün mit Moos sich
und Sternblumen im Gras
und goldene Sonnen auf Stengeln entstehn.

while in the fields
the weed of dissension is planted
and worn-out gardeners
let apples ripen on the moon!

But in the starry sky
the old man with the scales
weighs the weeping end
from the cloud to the worm!

Golem death!
But no one can lift you
out of time—
for the blood of your frenzy is borrowed
and your ironbound body
crumbles with all debris
back into the beginning!

But in the ruins dwells double longing!
The stone sleeps itself green with moss
and starwort in the grass
and golden suns on stems arise.

Und in den Wüsten
sieht man Schönes in der Ferne,
und wer die Braut verlor
umarmt die Luft,
denn nicht kann Geschaffenes ganz zugrunde gehn—

Und alle entgleisten Sterne
finden mit ihrem tiefsten Fall
immer zurück in das ewige Haus.

And in the deserts
beauty is seen in the distance,
and whoever lost the bride
embraces air,
for what was created cannot entirely perish—

And every star that fails
finds with its deepest fall
the way back to the eternal home.

—*Translated by Ruth and Matthew Mead*

Geschirmt sind die Liebenden

Geschirmt sind die Liebenden
unter dem zugemauerten Himmel.
Ein geheimes Element schafft ihnen Atem
und sie tragen die Steine in die Segnung
und alles was wächst
hat nur noch eine Heimat bei ihnen.

Geschirmt sind die Liebenden
und nur für sie schlagen noch die Nachtigallen
und sind nicht ausgestorben in der Taubheit
und des Waldes leise Legenden, die Rehe,
leiden in Sanftmut für sie.

Geschirmt sind die Liebenden
sie finden den versteckten Schmerz der Abendsonne
auf einem Weidenzweig blutend—
und üben in den Nächten lächelnd das Sterben,
den leisen Tod
mit allen Quellen, die in Sehnsucht rinnen.

The lovers are protected

The lovers are protected
beneath the walled-up sky.
A secret element gives them breath
and they bear the stones into the blessing
and all that grows
has a homeland only with them.

The lovers are protected
and only for them the nightingales sing
and have not died out in deafness
and the deer, soft legends of the forest,
suffer in meekness for them.

The lovers are protected
they find the hidden pain in the evening sun
bleeding on a willow branch—
and smilingly in the nights they practice dying
the quiet death
with all springs which run in longing.

—*Translated by Ruth and Matthew Mead*

Abraham

O du
aus dem mondversiegelten Ur,
der du im Sande der abtropfenden Sintfluthügel
die sausende Muschel
des Gottesgeheimnisses fandst—

O du
der du aus dem weinenden Sternbild Babylons
den Äon des lebenden Lebens hobst—
das Samenkorn des himmlischen Landmannes warfst
bis in den feurigen Abend des Heute darin die
    Ähre brennt.

O du
der aus Widderhörnern die neuen Jahrtausende
    geblasen
bis die Weltenecken sich bogen im Heimwehlaut—

Abraham

O you
out of moon-sealed Ur,
you who found the roaring seashell
of God's mystery
in the sand of the dune draining after the flood—

O you
who lifted the aeon of living life
from Babylon's weeping constellation—
cast the seed of the heavenly yeoman
even into this present fiery evening where the ear
    of corn is burning.

O you
who blew the new millennia from the rams' horns
until the corners of the world curved in a sound of
longing for home—

O du
der die Sehnsucht an den Horizont der unsichtbaren
    Himmel heftete
die Engel in die Länder der Nacht berief—
die Beete der Träume bereitete
für die Schar der sich übersteigenden Propheten—

O du
aus dessen ahnendem Blut
sich das Schmetterlingswort *Seele* entpuppte,
der auffliegende Wegweiser ins Ungesicherte hin—

O du
aus Chaldäas Sterndeuterhafen
unruhige Welle, die in unseren Adern
noch immer sucht voll Tränen ihr Meer.

O Abraham,
die Uhren aller Zeiten,
die sonnen- und monddurchleuchteten
hast du auf Ewigkeit gestellt—

O you
who nailed longing on the horizon
of invisible skies
called the angels into the lands of night—
who prepared the flowerbeds of dreams
for the troop of prophets outdoing each other—

O you
out of whose presaging blood
burst the butterfly word *soul,*
the signpost taking wing into incertitude—

O you
restless wave from Chaldea's
port of starry prophecy, which full of tears
still seeks its sea in our veins.

O Abraham
you have set at eternity
the clocks of all the ages,
lit by sun and moon—

O dein wunderbrennender Äon,
den wir mit unseren Leibern ans Ende bringen
   müssen—
dort, wo alle Reife hinfällt!

O your aeon burning with wonders
which we with our bodies must consummate—
there, where all ripeness falls!

—*Translated by Ruth and Matthew Mead*

Jakob

O Israel,
Erstling im Morgengrauenkampf
wo alle Geburt mit Blut
auf der Dämmerung geschrieben steht.
O das spitze Messer des Hahnenschreis
der Menschheit ins Herz gestochen,
o die Wunde zwischen Nacht und Tag
die unser Wohnort ist!

Vorkämpfer,
im kreissenden Fleisch der Gestirne
in der Nachtwachentrauer
daraus ein Vogellied weint.

O Israel,
du einmal zur Seligkeit endlich Entbundener—
des Morgentaus tröpfelnde Gnade
auf deinem Haupt—

Jacob

O Israel,
Firstborn in the grapple of gray morning
where all birth is written with blood
upon the dawn.
O the pointed knife of cockcrow
thrust in the heart of mankind,
O the wound between night and day
which is our dwelling place!

Champion,
in the travailing flesh of constellations
in the sorrow of the nightwatch
from which a birdsong weeps.

O Israel
you born at last to bliss—
the dripping grace of the morning dew
upon your head—

Seliger für uns,
die in Vergessenheit Verkauften,
ächzend im Treibeis
von Tod und Auferstehung

und vom schweren Engel über uns
zu Gott verrenkt
wie du!

More blissful for us,
sold in forgetfulness,
groaning in the drifting ice
of death and resurrection

and disabled to God
by the heavy angel above us
like you!

  —*Translated by Ruth and Matthew Mead*

Wenn die Propheten einbrächen

Wenn die Propheten einbrächen
durch Türen der Nacht,
den Tierkreis der Dämonengötter
wie einen schauerlichen Blumenkranz
ums Haupt gewunden—
die Geheimnisse der stürzenden und sich hebenden
Himmel mit den Schultern wiegend—

für die längst vom Schauer Fortgezogenen—

Wenn die Propheten einbrächen
durch Türen der Nacht,
die Sternenstrassen gezogen in ihren Handflächen
golden aufleuchten lassend—

für die längst im Schlaf Versunkenen—

Wenn die Propheten einbrächen
durch Türen der Nacht
mit ihren Worten Wunden reissend

If the prophets broke in

If the prophets broke in
through the doors of night,
the zodiac of demon gods
wound like a ghastly wreath of flowers
round the head—
rocking the secrets of the falling and rising
skies on their shoulders—

for those who long since fled in terror—

If the prophets broke in
through the doors of night,
the course of the stars scored in their palms
glowing golden—

for those long sunk in sleep—

If the prophets broke in
through the doors of night
tearing wounds with their words

in die Felder der Gewohnheit,
ein weit Entlegenes hereinholend
für den Tagelöhner

der längst nicht mehr wartet am Abend—

Wenn die Propheten einbrächen
durch Türen der Nacht
und ein Ohr wie eine Heimat suchten—

Ohr der Menschheit
du nesselverwachsenes,
würdest du hören?
Wenn die Stimme der Propheten
auf dem Flötengebein der ermordeten Kinder
blasen würde,
die vom Märtyrerschrei verbrannten Lüfte
ausatmete—
wenn sie eine Brücke aus verendeten Greisenseufzern
baute—

Ohr der Menschheit
du mit dem kleinen Lauschen beschäftigtes,
würdest du hören?

into fields of habit,
a distant crop hauled home
for the laborer

who no longer waits at evening—

If the prophets broke in
through the doors of night
and sought an ear like a homeland—

Ear of mankind
overgrown with nettles,
would you hear?
If the voice of the prophets
blew
on flutes made of murdered children's bones
and exhaled airs burnt with
martyrs' cries—
if they built a bridge of old men's dying
groans—

Ear of mankind
occupied with small sounds,
would you hear?

Wenn die Propheten
Mit den Sturmschwingen der Ewigkeit hineinführen
wenn sie aufbrächen deinen Gehörgang mit
    den Worten:
Wer von euch will Krieg führen gegen ein Geheimnis
wer will den Sterntod erfinden?

Wenn die Propheten aufständen
in der Nacht der Menschheit
wie Liebende, die das Herz des Geliebten suchen,
Nacht der Menschheit
würdest du ein Herz zu vergeben haben?

If the prophets
rushed in with the storm-pinions of eternity
it they broke open your acoustic duct with the words:
Which of you wants to make war against a mystery
who wants to invent the star-death?

If the prophets stood up
in the night of mankind
like lovers who seek the heart of the beloved,
night of mankind
would you have a heart to offer?

    —Translated by Ruth and Matthew Mead

Hiob

O du Windrose der Qualen!
Von Urzeitstürmen
in immer andere Richtungen der Unwetter gerissen;
noch dein Süden heisst Einsamkeit.
Wo du stehst, ist der Nabel der Schmerzen.

Deine Augen sind tief in deinen Schädel gesunken
wie Höhlentauben in der Nacht
die der Jäger blind herausholt.
Deine Stimme ist stumm geworden,
denn sie hat zuviel *Warum* gefragt.

Zu den Würmern und Fischen ist deine Stimme
    eingegangen.
Hiob, du hast alle Nachtwachen durchweint
aber einmal wird das Sternbild deines Blutes
alle aufgehenden Sonnen erbleichen lassen.

Job

O you windrose of agonies!
Swept by primordial storms
always into other directions of inclemency;
even your South is called loneliness.
Where you stand is the navel of pain.

Your eyes have sunk deep into your skull
like cave doves which the hunter
fetches blindly at night.
Your voice has gone dumb,
having too often asked *why*.

Your voice has joined the worms and fishes.
Job, you have cried through all vigils
but one day the constellation of your blood
shall make all rising suns blanch.

—*Translated by Michael Roloff*

Daniel

Daniel, Daniel—
die One ihres Sterbens
sind in meinem Schlaf erwacht—
dort, wo ihre Qual mit dem Welken der Haut verging
haben die Steine die Wunde
ihrer abgebrochenen Zeit gewiesen—
haben sich die Bäume ausgerissen
die mit ihren Wurzeln
die Verwandlung des Staubes
zwischen Heute und Morgen fassen.

Sind die Verliese mit ihren erstickten Schreien
aufgebrochen,
die mit ihrer stummen Gewalt
den neuen Stern gebären helfen—
ist der Weg mit den Hieroglyphen ihrer Fusspuren
in meine Ohren gerieselt
wie in Stundenuhren,
die der Tod erst wendet.

Daniel

Daniel, Daniel—
the places where they died
have awakened in my sleep—
there, where their torment passed from them as their
    skin wrinkled,
stones have shown the wounds
of their discontinued time—
the trees have torn themselves up
which with their roots
clutch the metamorphosis of dust
between today and tomorrow.

Are the dungeons broken open
by their suffocated cries,
which help to give birth to the new star
with their dumb force—
has the way with the hieroglyphics of their footprints
trickled into my ears
as in hourglasses
which are only turned by death.

O die gräberlosen Seufzer in der Luft,
die sich in unseren Atem schleichen—
Daniel, Daniel,
wo bist du schreckliches Traumlicht?
Der ungedeuteten Zeichen sind zu viele geworden—

O wir Quellenlose,
die wir keine Mündung mehr verstehn,
wenn sich das Samenkorn im Tode
des Lebens erinnert—

Daniel, Daniel,
vielleicht stehst du zwischen Leben und Tod
in der Küche, wo in deinem Schein
auf dem Tische liegt
der Fisch mit den ausgerissenen Purpurkiemen,
ein König des Schmerzes?

O the graveless sighs in the air
which creep into our breath-
Daniel, Daniel,
where are you terrible dreamlight?
The uninterpreted signs have become too many—

O we without a source,
we who understand a mouth no more,
when the seed in death
remembers life—

Daniel, Daniel,
perhaps you stand between life and death
in the kitchen, where in your light
the fish with the torn-out purple gills
lies on the table,
a king of pain?

—*Translated by Ruth and Matthew Mead*

Aber deine Brunnen

Aber deine Brunnen
sind deine Tagebücher
o Israel!

Wieviel Münder hast du geöffnet
im vertrockneten Sand,
die Scheibe des Todes abgeschnitten
vom lebenden Leben.

Wieviel leuchtende Wurzeln der Sehnsucht
hast du aus der Tiefe gehoben
wieviel Gestirnen hast du Spiegel aufgetan,
ihr Geschmeide in den dunkel
weinenden Schlaf gelegt.

Denn deine Brunnen
sind deine Tagebücher
o Israel!

But your wells

But your wells
are your book of days
O Israel!

How many mouths have you opened
in the parched sand,
the slice of death cut off
from living life.

How many glowing roots of longing
have you lifted from the depth
for how many constellations have you opened mirrors,
laying their jewelry into the dark
weeping sleep.

For your wells
are your book of days
O Israel!

Als Abraham grub in Ber Seba
heftete er mit sieben Schwüren
den Namen seines Herrn
in die Heimat des Wassers.

Ihr, durch das Fleisch der Erde Dürstenden,
viele Begegnungen sind euch aufbewahrt
im fliessenden Gebetschrein der Brunnen.
Gesicht des Engels
über Hagars Schulter geneigt
wie eine Nebelhaut
ihren Tod fortblasend.

Redender Fels mit der bitteren
Wasserzunge zu Mara,
die mit verlorenem Geheimnis getaucht
zur Süsse sich wandelte—

Deine Tagebücher
sind in die leuchtenden Augen
der Wüsten geschrieben
o Israel!

When Abraham dug in Beersheba
he nailed the name of his god
with seven oaths
into the home of water.

You who thirst through the flesh of earth,
many encounters are preserved for you
in the wells' flowing shrine of prayer.
The angel's face
bending over Hagar's shoulder
blowing her death away
like a skin of mist.

Rock speaking to Mara
with the bitter tongue of water
which dipped with a lost secret
changed to sweetness—

Your book of days
is written into the shining eyes
of the deserts
O Israel!

Schlagrutenhaft
dein Herz zuckt
wo die Schalen der Nacht
eine Brunnentiefe halten,
darunter die Landschaften Gottes
zu blühen beginnen,
die du, Erinnernder unter den Völkern,
hinaufhebst
mit dern Krug deines Herzens—
hinaufhebst
in die brunnenlosen Räume
der Vergessenheit!

As if struck by a rod
your heart quivers
where the bowls of night
hold the depths of a well
beneath which the landscapes of God
begin to bloom,
which you, rememberer among the nations,
lift up
with the vessel of your heart—
lift up
into the spaces of forgetfulness
where no wells are!

—*Translated by Ruth and Matthew Mead*

Warum die schwarze Antwort des Hasses

Warum die schwarze Antwort des Hasses
auf dein Dasein, Israel?

Fremdling du,
einen Stern von weiterher
als die anderen.
Verkauft an diese Erde
damit Einsamkeit fort sich erbe.

Deine Herkunft verwachsen mit Unkraut—
deine Sterne vertauscht
gegen alles was Motten und Würmern gehört,
und doch von den Traumsandufern der Zeit
wie Mondwasser fortgeholt in die Ferne.

Im Chore der anderen
hast du gesungen
einen Ton höher
oder einen Ton tiefer—

Why the black answer of hate

Why the black answer of hate
to your existence, Israel?

You stranger
from a star one farther away
than the others.
Sold to this earth
that loneliness might be passed on.

Your origin entangled in weeds—
your stars bartered
for all that belongs to moths and worms,
and yet: fetched away from dreamfilled sandy
    shores of time
like moonwater into the distance.

In the others' choir
you always sang
one note lower
or one note higher—

der Abendsonne hast du dich ins Blut geworfen
wie ein Schmerz den anderen sucht.
Lang ist dein Schatten
und es ist späte Zeit fur dich geworden
Israel!

Wie weit dein Weg von der Segnung
den Äon der Tränen entlang
bis zu der Wegbiegung
da du in Asche gefallen,

dein Feind mit dem Rauch
deines verbrannten Leibes
deine Todverlassenheit
an die Stirn des Himmels schrieb!

O solcher Tod!
Wo alle helfenden Engel
mit blutenden Schwingen
zerrissen im Stacheldraht
der Zeit hingen!

you flung yourself into the blood of the evening sun
like one pain seeking the other.
Long is your shadow
and it has become late for you
Israel!

How far your way from the blessing
along the aeon of tears
to the bend of the road
where you turned to ashes

and your enemy with the smoke
of your burned body
engraved your mortal abandonment
on the brow of heaven!

O such a death!
When all helping angels
with bleeding wings
hung tattered
in the barbed wire of time!

Warum die schwarze Antwort des Hasses
auf dein Dasein
Israel?

Why the black answer of hate
to your existence
Israel?

—*Translated by Michael Roloff*

Sinai

Du Truhe des Sternschlafs
aufgebrochen in der Nacht,
wo alle deine Schätze,
die versteinten Augen der Liebenden,
ihre Münder, Ohren, ihr verwestes Glück
in die Herrlichkeit gerieten.
Rauchend vor Erinnerung schlugst du aus
da die Hand der Ewigkeit deine Sanduhr wendete—
die Libelle im Bluteisenstein
ihre Schöpferstunde wusste—

Sinai
von deinem Gipfel
Moses trug,
schrittweise abkühlend
den geöffneten Himmel
an seiner Stirn herab,
bis die im Schatten Harrenden
das unter dem schützenden Tuche Brodelnde
schauernd ertrugen—

Sinai

You ark of starry sleep
broken open in the night,
where all your treasures,
the petrified eyes of the lovers,
their mouths, ears, their putrefied happiness
moved into glory.
Smoking with memory you struck out
as the hand of eternity turned your hourglass—
as the dragonfly in the blood-ironstone
knew the hour of its creator—

Sinai
down from your peak
Moses bore the opened sky
on his forehead
cooling step by step
until they who waited in the shadow
were able to bear, trembling,
what shone beneath the veil—

Wo ist noch ein Abkömmling
aus der Erschauerten Nachfolge?
O so leuchte er auf
im Haufen der Erinnerungslosen,
Versteinten!

Is there still an heir
to the succession of them that trembled?
Oh, may he glow
in the crowd of them that do not remember,
of the petrified!

—*Translated by Ruth and Matthew Mead*

David

Samuel sah
hinter der Blindenbinde des Horizontes—
Samuel sah—
im Entscheidungsbereich
wo die Gestirne entbrennen, versinken,
David den Hirten
durcheilt von Sphärenmusik.
Wie Bienen näherten sich ihm die Sterne
Honig ahnend—

Als die Männer ihn suchten
tanzte er, umraucht
von der Lämmer Schlummerwolle,
bis er stand
und sein Schatten auf einen Widder fiel—

David

Samuel saw
behind the blindfold of the horizon—
Samuel saw—
in the realm of decision,
where the constellations ignite, sink,
David the shepherd
quickened by music of the spheres.
The stars came to him like bees
sensing honey—

As the men sought him
he danced, surrounded by smoke
from the lambs' sleepy wool,
till he stood
and his shadow fell on a ram—

Da hatte die Königszeit begonnen—
Aber im Mannesjahr
mass er, ein Vater der Dichter,
in Verzweiflung
die Entfernung zu Gott aus,
und baute der Psalmen Nachtherbergen
für die Wegwunden.

Sterbend hatte er mehr Verworfenes
dem Würmertod zu geben
als die Schar seiner Väter—
Denn von Gestalt zu Gestalt
weint sich der Engel im Menschen
tiefer in das Licht!

The age of kings had begun—
But in the year he came of age
he measured out in despair,
a father of poets,
the distance to God,
and built inns of night from the psalms
for those left by the way.

Dying he had more depravity
to give to wormy death
than all his forefathers—
For from form to form
the angel in man weeps itself
deeper into the light!

—*Translated by Ruth and Matthew Mead*

Saul

Saul, der Herrscher, abgeschnitten vom Geiste
wie eine Brennschnur erloschen—

Einen Fächer von Fragen tragend in der Hand—
das Wahrsageweib mit der Antwort, auf Nachtgaloschen

beunruhigt den Sand.
Und Samuels, des Propheten Stimme,

gerissen aus dem Lichterkreis
spricht wie verwelkte Erinnerung in die Luft—

und das Licht wie eine verzückte Imme
sein Ausgefahrnes in die Ewigkeit ruft.

Über Saul, dem Herrscher, steht eine Krone
    aus Sterben—
und das Weib liegt wie vom Lichte verbrannt—

und die Macht wird ein armer Luftzug erben
und legt sie zu einem Haupteshaar in den Sand.

Saul

Saul, the ruler, cut off from the spirit
extinguished like a burning fuse—

Carrying a fan of questions in the hand—
the witch with the answer, in night shoes

disturbs the sand.
And Samuel's, the voice of prophecy,

torn from the circle of lights
speaks like a withered memory into the air—

and the light like an ecstatic bee
calls into eternity his soul that was elsewhere.

Above Saul, the ruler, hangs a crown of dying—
and the woman lies as if burnt by the light's glare—

And a poor breeze, heir to the power, will lay it sighing
into the sand beside a single hair.

—Translated by Ruth and Matthew Mead

Israel

Israel,
namenloser einst,
noch von des Todes Efeu umsponnen,
arbeitete geheim die Ewigkeit in dir, traumtief
bestiegst du
der Mondtürme magische Spirale,
die mit Tiermasken verhüllten Gestirne
umkreisend—
in der Fische Mirakelstummheit
oder mit des Widders anstürmender Härte.

Bis der versiegelte Himmel aufbrach
und du,
Waghalsigster unter den Nachtwandlern,
getroffen von der Gotteswunde
in den Abgrund aus Licht fielst—

Israel

Israel,
more nameless then,
still ensnared in the ivy of death,
in you eternity worked secretly, dream-deep
you mounted
the enchanted spiral of the moon towers,
circling the constellations disguised
by animal masks—
in the mute miraculous silence of Pisces
or the battering charges of Aries.

Until the sealed sky broke open
and you,
most daredevil of sleepwalkers,
fell, struck by the wound of God
into the abyss of light—

Israel,
Zenit der Sehnsucht,
gehäuft über deinem Haupte
ist das Wunder wie Gewitter,
entlädt sich im Schmerzgebirge deiner Zeit.

Israel,
erst zart, wie das Lied der Vögel
und leidender Kinder Gespräche
rinnt des lebendigen Gottes Quelle
heimatlich aus deinem Blut—

Israel,
zenith of longing,
wonder is heaped
like a storm upon your head,
breaks in your time's mountains of pain.

Israel,
tender at first, like the song of a bird
and the talk of suffering children
the source of the living God,
a native spring,
flows from your blood.

—Translated by Michael Roloff

Geheime Grabschrift

O welche Rune schreibt der Erdenschoss
mit einer Eiche qualverbogenem Geäst
in diese Luft, die Zeit mit Schreckenmuster malt.

Greis mit dem Kaftan—
Mantel aus der grossen Einsamkeit geschnitten,
von vielen Tod- und Weihekerzen angeraucht—
Greis in der heimatlosesten der Sprachen seufzend—

Der eiserne Soldat liess dich in Wellen
an dem Baume leiden
nachschaffend eine windverrenkte Erdennucht.

Zenit des Schmerzes!
Harfend Tränenholz
und Krähen die den Sterbebissen kauen
den Grausamkeit noch übrig liess—

Secret Epitaph

Oh, what rune does the womb of earth
inscribe with an oak's torment-twisted branches
upon this air, which paints time with patterns of terror.

Old man with the caftan—
Coat cut from the great loneliness,
smoky with many candles of death and consecration—
Old man sighing in the most homeless of languages—

The iron soldier let you suffer in waves
at the tree,
re-creating a wind-twisted flight from earth.

Zenith of pain!
Wooden harp of tears
and crows chewing the morsel of death
which cruelty left over—

Vielleicht ist hier die Stelle
wo dieser Stern, die schwarzversiegelte
Geheimnisfülle sprengt
und furchtbar überkocht
in unfassbare Ewigkeit hinein!

Perhaps this is the place
where this star will burst the black-sealed
abundance of secrets
and boil over monstrously
into inconceivable eternity!

—Translated by Ruth and Matthew Mead

Zahlen

Als eure Formen zu Asche versanken
in die Nachtmeere,
wo Ewigkeit in die Gezeiten
Leben und Tod spült—

erhoben sich Zahlen—
(gebrannt einmal in eure Arme
damit niemand der Qual entginge)

erhoben sich Meteore aus Zahlen,
gerufen in die Räume
darin Lichterjahre wie Pfeile sich strecken
und die Planeten
aus den magischen Stoffen
des Schmerzes geboren werden—

Zahlen—mit ihren Wurzeln
aus Mördergehirnen gezogen
und schon eingerechnet
in des himmlischen Kreislaufs
blaugeäderter Bahn.

Numbers

When your forms turned to ashes
into the oceans of night
where eternity washes
life and death into the tides—

there rose the numbers—
(once branded into your arms
so none would escape the agony)

there rose meteors of numbers
beckoned into the spaces
where light-years expand like arrows
and the planets
are born
of the magic substances of pain—

numbers—root and all
plucked out of murderers' brains
and part already
of the heavenly cycle's
path of blue veins.

—*Translated by Michael Roloff*

Greise

Da,
in den Falten dieses Sterns,
zugedeckt mit einem Fetzen Nacht,
stehen sie, und warten Gott ab.
Ihr Mund hat ein Dorn verschlossen,
ihre Sprache ist an ihre Augen verlorengegangen,
die reden wie Brunnen
darin ein Leichnam ertrunken ist.
O die Alten,
die ihre verbrannte Nachfolge in den Augen tragen
als einzigen Besitz.

Old men

There
in the folds of this star
covered with tatters of night
they stand and wait for God.
A thorn has closed their mouths,
they speak only with their eyes,
they speak like a well
in which a corpse has drowned.
O the old men
who carry their burnt succession in their eyes
as their sole possession.

—*Translated by Ruth and Matthew Mead*

Welt, frage nicht die Todentrissenen

Welt, frage nicht die Todentrissenen
wohin sie gehen,
sie gehen immer ihrem Grabe zu.
Das Pflaster der fremden Stadt
war nicht für die Musik von Flüchtlingsschritten
    gelegt worden—
Die Fenster der Häuser, die eine Erdenzeit spiegeln
mit den wandernden Gabentischen
    der Bilderbuchhimmel—
wurden nicht für Augen geschliffen
die den Schrecken an seiner Quelle tranken.
Welt, die Fake ihres Lächelns hat ihnen ein
    starkes Eisen ausgebrannt;
sie möchten so gerne zu dir kommen
um deiner Schönheit wegen,
aber wer heimatlos ist, dem welken alle Wege
wie Schnittblumen hin—

World, do not ask those snatched from death

World, do not ask those snatched from death
where they are going,
they are always going to their graves.
The pavements of the foreign city
were not laid for the music of fugitive footsteps—
The windows of the houses that reflect a lifetime
of shifting tables heaped with gifts from a picture-book
   heaven—
were not cut for eyes
which drank terror at its source.
World, a strong iron has cauterized the wrinkle of
   their smile;
they would like to come to you
because of your beauty,
but for the homeless all ways wither
like cut flowers—

Aber, es ist uns in der Fremde
eine Freundin geworden: die Abendsonne.
Eingesegnet von ihrem Marterlicht
sind wir geladen zu ihr zu kommen mit unserer Trauer,
die neben uns geht:
Ein Psalm der Nacht.

But we have found a friend
in exile: the evening sun.
Blessed by its suffering light
we are bidden to come to it with our sorrow
which walks beside us:
A psalm of night.

—*Translated by Ruth and Matthew Mead*

Wir sind so wund

Wir sind so wund,
dass wir zu sterben glauben
wenn die Gasse uns ein böses Wort nachwirft.
Die Gasse weiss es nicht,
aber sie erträgt nicht eine solche Belastung;
nicht gewöhnt ist sie einen Vesuv der Schmerzen
auf ihr ausbrechen zu sehn.
Die Erinnerungen an Urzeiten sind ausgetilgt bei ihr,
seitdem das Licht künstlich wurde
und die Engel nur noch mit Vögeln und Blumen spielen
oder im Traume eines Kindes lächeln.

We are so stricken

We are so stricken
that we think we're dying
when the street casts an evil word at us.
The street does not know it,
but it cannot stand such a weight;
it is not used to seeing a Vesuvius of pain
break out.
Its memories of primeval times are obliterated,
since the light became artificial
and angels only play with birds and flowers
or smile in a child's dream.

—Translated by Ruth and Matthew Mead

Auf den Landstraßen der Erde

Auf den Landstrassen der Erde
liegen die Kinder
mit den Wurzeln
aus der Muttererde gerissen.
Das licht der erloschenen Liebe
ist ihrer Hand entfallen
deren Leere sich mit Wind füllt.

Wenn der Vater aller Waisen,
der Abend, mit ihnen
aus allen Wunden blutet
und ihre zitternden Schatten
die herzzerreissende Angst
ihrer Leiber abmalen—
fallen sie plötzlich hinab in de Nacht
wie in den Tod.

Aber im Schmerzgebirge der Morgendämmerung
sterben ihnen Vater und Mutter
wieder und immer wieder.

The Children lie

The children lie
on all the roads of earth
torn by the roots
from mother earth.
The light of extinguished love
has fallen from their hands,
wind fills the empty hands.

When evening, father
of all orphans, bleeds
with them from all wounds
and their trembling shadows
mimic the heartbreaking fear
of their bodies—
they plunge suddenly into night
as though into death.

But at dawn in the hills of pain
they see their fathers and mothers
dying again and again.

—*Translated by Ruth and Matthew Mead*

O die Heimatlosen Farben des Abendhimmels!

O die Heimatlosen Farben des Abendhimmels!
O die Blüten des Sterbens in den Wolken
wie der Neugeborenen Verbleichen!

O der Schwalben Rätselfragen
an das Geheimnis—
der Möven entmenschter Schrei
aus der Schöpfungszeit—

Woher wir Übriggebliebenen aus Sternverdunkelung?
Woher wir mit dem Licht über dem Haupte
dessen Schatten Tod uns anmalt?

Die Zeit rauscht von unserem Heimweh
wie eine Muschel

und das Feuer in der Tiefe der Erde
weiss schon um unseren Zerfall—

O the homeless colors of the evening sky!

O the homeless colors of the evening sky!
O the blossoms of death in the clouds
like the pale dying of the newly born!

O the riddles that the swallows
ask the mystery—
the inhuman cry of the gulls
from the day of creation—

Whence we survivors of the stars' darkening?
Whence we with the light above our heads
whose shadow death paints on us?

Time roars with our longing for home
like a seashell

and the fire in the depths of the earth
already knows of our ruin—

—Translated by Ruth and Matthew Mead

Wir Mütter

Wir Mütter,
Sehnsuchtsamen aus Meeresnacht
holen wir heim,
Heimholerinnen sind wir
von verstreutem Gut.

Wir Mütter,
träumerisch
mit den Gestirnen wandelnd,
lassen uns die Fluten
von Gestern und Morgen,
mit unserer Geburt
wie mit einer Insel
allein.

Wir Mütter
die wir zum Tode sagen:
Blühe auf in unserem Blut.
Die wir Sand zum Lieben bringen
und den Sternen eine spiegelnde Welt—

We mothers

We mothers,
we gather seed of desire
from oceanic night,
we are gatherers
of scattered goods.

We mothers,
pacing dreamily
with the constellations,
the floods
of past and future,
leave us alone
with our birth
like an island.

We mothers
who say to death:
blossom in our blood.
We who impel sand to love and bring
a mirroring world to the stars—

Wir Mütter,
die wir in den Wiegen
die dämmernden Erinnerungen
des Schöpfertages wiegen—
des Atemzuges Auf und Ab
ist unseres Liebessanges Melodie.

Wir Mütter
wiegen in das Herz der Welt
die Friedensmelodie.

We mothers,
who rock in the cradles
the shadowy memories
of creation's day—
the to and fro of each breath
is the melody of our love long.

We mothers
rock into the heart of the world
the melody of peace.

—*Translated by Ruth and Matthew Mead*

Immer

Immer
dort wo Kinder sterben
werden die leisesten Dinge heimatlos.
Der Schmerzensmantel der Abendröte
darin die dunkle Seele der Amsel
die Nacht heranklagt—
kleine Winde über zitternde Gräser hinwehend
die Trümmer des Lichtes verlöschend
und Sterben säend—

Immer
dort wo Kinder sterben
verbrennen die Feuergesichter
der Nacht, einsam in ihrem Geheimnis—
Und wer weiss von den Wegweisern
die der Tod ausschickt:
Geruch des Lebensbaumes,
Hahnenschrei der den Tag verkürzt
Zauberuhr vom Grauen des Herbstes
in die Kinderstuben hinein verwunschen—

Always

Always
there where children die
the quietest things become homeless.
The sunset's cloak of pain
in which the blackbird's dark soul
sadly heralds the night—
small winds blowing across trembling grasses
extinguishing the debris of light
and sowing death—

Always
there where children die
the fiery faces of the night
burn out, lonely in their mystery—
And who knows of the signposts
that death sends out:
smell of the tree of life,
cockcrow that shortens the day
magic clock enchanted into nurseries
by the horror of autumn—

Spülen der Wasser an die Ufer des Dunkels
rauschender, ziehender Schlaf der Zeit—

Immer
dort wo Kinder sterben
verhängen sich die Spiegel der Puppenhäuser
mit einem Hauch,
sehen nicht mehr den Tanz der Fingerliliputaner
in Kmderblutatlas gekleidet;
Tanz der stille steht
wie erne im Fernglas
mondentrückte Welt.

Immer
dort wo Kinder sterben
werden Stein und Stern
und so viele Träume
heimatlos.

water lapping on the shore of darkness
whispering, tugging sleep of time—

Always
there where children die
doll's house mirrors cloud over
with a breath,
see no more the dance of the finger-midgets
clad in child's-blood satin;
dance that stands still
like a world in a telescope
shifted to the moon.

Always
there where children die
stone and star
and so many dreams
become homeless.

  —*Translated by Ruth and Matthew Mead*

Trauernde Mutter

Nach der Wüste des Tages,
in der Oase des Abends,
über die Brücke welche
die Liebe sich über zwei Welten weinte,
kam dein toter Knabe.
Alle deine versunkenen Luftschlösser
die Scherben deiner flammenversehrten Paläste,
Gesänge und Segnungen
untergegangen in deiner Trauer,
umfunkeln ihn wie eine Feste,
die der Tod nicht eingenommen hat.

Sein milchbetauter Mund,
seine Hand, die deine überholt hat,
sein Schatten an der Zimmerwand
ein Flügel der Nacht,
mit der gelöschten Lampe heimwärtssinkend—
am Strande zu Gott
hingestreut wie Vogelbrocken in ein Meer
des Kindesgebetes Echolaut
und übern Rand des Schlafs gefallener Kuss—

Mourning Mother

After the desert of day,
in the oasis of evening,
your dead boy came
across the bridge
which love had wept between two worlds.
All your sunken castles in air
the shards of your flame-seared palaces,
songs and blessings
drowned in your sorrow,
sparkled around him like a fortress
unconquered by death.

His milk-bedewed mouth,
his hand which has outreached yours,
his shadow on the wall of the room
a wing of night,
sinking homewards with the extinguished lamp
strewn for God
on the shore like crumbs for birds into a sea
the echo of the child's prayer
and the kiss fallen over the rim of sleep—

O Mutter, Erinnernde,
nichts ist mehr dein
und alles—
denn die stürzenden Sterne suchen
durch die Mohnfelder der Vergessenheit
auf ihrem Heimweg dein Herz,
denn alle deine Empfängnis
ist hilfloses Leid.

O mother, rememberer,
nothing more is yours
and everything—
for the falling stars on their way home
search for your heart
in the poppy fields of oblivion,
for all your conceiving
is helpless suffering.

—*Translated by Ruth and Matthew Mead*

Abschied

Abschied—
aus zwei Wunden blutendes Wort.
Gestern noch Meereswort
mit dem sinkenden Schiff
als Schwert in der Mitte—
Gestern noch von Sternschnuppensterben
durchstochenes Wort—
Mitternachtogeküsste Kehle
der Nachtigallen—

Heute—zwei hängenden Fetzen
und Menschenhaar in einer Krallenhand
die riss—

Und wir Nachblutenden—
Verblutende an dir—
halten deine Quelle in unseren Händen.
Wir Heerscharen der Abschiednehmenden
die an deiner Dunkelheit bauen—
bis der Tod sagt: schweige du—
doch hier ist: weiterbluten!

Farewell

Farewell—
word bleeding from two wounds.
Yesterday still a word of the sea
with the sinking ship
as sword in the middle—
Yesterday still a word
pierced by the dying of shooting stars—
midnight-kissed throat
of the nightingales—

Today—two hanging shreds
and human hair in a clawing hand
that tore—

And we who bleed in aftermath—
bleeding to death because of you—
hold your source in our hands.
We hosts who bid farewell
who build your darkness—
until death says: be silent—
but here it is: go on bleeding!

—*Translated by Ruth and Matthew Mead*

Land Israel

Land Israel,
deine Weite, ausgemessen einst
van deinen, den Horizont übersteigenden Heiligen
Deine Morgenluft besprochen von den
    Erstlingen Gottes,
deine Berge, deine Büsche
aufgegangen im Flammenatem
des turchtbar nahegerückten Geheimnisses.

Land Israel,
erwählte Sternenstätte
für den himmlischen Kuss!

Land Israel,
nun wo dein vom Sterben angebranntes Volk
einzieht in deine Täler
und alle Echos den Erzvätersegen rufen
für die Rückkehrer,
ihnen kündend, wo im schattenlosen Licht
Elia mit dem Landmanne ging zusammen am Pfluge,
der Ysop im Garten wuchs

Land of Israel

Land of Israel,
your bounds once measured out
by your saints surmounting the horizon.
Your morning air enchanted by God's firstborn,
your mountains, your bushes
gone up in the breath of flame
of the terribly close-come mystery.

Land of Israel,
chosen starry place
for the celestial kiss!

Land of Israel,
now when your people seared by dying
move into your valleys
and all echoes call the patriarchs' blessing
for those returning,
proclaiming to them where in the shadowless light
Elijah walked with the yeoman at the plow,
where hyssop grew in the garden

und schon an der Mauer des Paradieses—
wo die schmale Gasse gelaufen zwischen Hier und Dort
da, wo Er gab und nahm als Nachbar
und der Tod keines Erntewagens bedurfte.

Land Israel,
nun wo dein Volk
aus den Weltenecken verweint heimkommt
urn die Psalmen Davids neu zu schreiben in
    deinen Sand
und das Feierabendwort *Vollbracht*
am Abend seiner Ernte singt—

steht vielleicht schon eine nene Ruth
in Armut ihre Lese haltend
am Scheidewege ihrer Wanderschaft.

and even by the wall of paradise—
where the small alley ran between here and there
there where He gave and took as neighbor
and death needed no cart for harvest.

Land of Israel,
now when your people
come home from the corners of the world with
   tear-stained eyes
to write the psalms of David anew in your sand
and that afterwork word *finished*
sings on the evening of its harvest—

perhaps a new Ruth is already standing
in poverty holding her gleanings
at the crossroad of her wandering.

   —Translated by Ruth and Matthew Mead

Nun hat Abraham die Wurzel
der Winde gefaßt

Nun hat Abraham die Wurzel der Winde gefasst
denn heimkehren wird Israel aus der Zerstreuung.

Eingesammelt hat es Wunden und Martern
auf den Höfen der Welt,
abgeweint alle verschlossenen Türen.

Seine Alten, den Erdenkleidern fast entwachsen
und wie Meerpflanzen die Glieder streckend,

einbalsamiert im Salze der Verzweiflung
und die Klagemauer Nacht im Arm—
werden noch einen kleinen Schlat tun—

Aber die Jungen haben die Sehnsuchtsfahne entfaltet,
denn ein Acker will von ihnen geliebt werden
und eine Wüste getränkt

Now Abraham has seized the root of the winds

Now Abraham has seized the root of the winds
for home shall Israel come from the dispersion.

It has gathered wounds and afflictions
in the courtyards of the world,
has bathed all locked doors with its tears.

Its elders, having almost outgrown their earthly garb
and extending their limbs like sea plants,

embalmed in the salt of despair
and the wailing wall night in their arms—
will sleep just a spell longer—

But youth has unfurled its flag of longing,
for a field yearns to be loved by them
and a desert watered

und nach der Sonnenseite Gott
sollen die Häuser gebaut werden

und der Abend hat wieder das veilchenscheue Wort,
das nur in der Heimat so blau bereitet wird:
Gute Nacht!

and the house shall be built
to face the sun: God

and evening again has the violet-shy word
that only grows so blue in the homeland:
Good night!

—*Translated by Michael Roloff*

Aus dem Wüstensand

Aus dem Wüstensand holst du deine Wohnstatt
   wieder heim.
Aus den Jahrtausenden, die liegen in
   Goldsand verwandelt.

Aus dem Wüstensand treibst du deine Bäume
   wieder hoch
die nehmen die Quellen hin zu den Sternen—

Aus dem Wüstensand in den soviel Schlaf einging
vom Volke Israel

ziehst du der Schafe Schlummerwolle an den Tag.
Mit der Erinnerung als Rutengänger

gräbst du die versteckten Blitze der
   Gottesgewitter aus,
wälzt die Steine zum Bethaus

Out of the desert sand

Out of the desert sand you bring your dwelling
    place home again.
Out of the millennia which lie transformed in sand
    of gold.

Out of the desert sand you thrust up your trees again
they take the wells up to the stars—

Out of the desert sand into which so much sleep
of Israel's people entered

you draw the sleepy wool of sheep to the light.
With memory as dowser

you dig out the hidden lightnings of God's storms,
roll the stones to the temple

Steine, die fester Schlaf um die magische Nacht
von Beth-El sind,

und gefrorene Zeit um der Heimwehleitern Gespross.
Am Abend aber, wenn die Erde ihre letzte Melodie

am Horizont spielt und die Brunnen dunkle
    Rahelaugen sind,
öffnet Abraham den blauen Himmelsschrein

darin die funkelnde Tiara des Tierkreises ruht,
Israels ewige Siegertrophäe

an die schlafenden Völker der Welt.

stones, which are deep sleep around the magic night
of Beth-el,

and frozen time around the ladder rungs
    of homesickness.
But at evening when earth plays its last melody

on the horizon and the wells are dark eyes of Rachel
Abraham opens the blue shrine of the sky

in which the sparkling tiara of the zodiac rests,
Israel's eternal trophy of victory

to the sleeping peoples of the world.

   —*Translated by Ruth and Matthew Mead*

Frauen und Mädchen Israels

Frauen und Mädchen Israels,
das mit dem Schlafstrauch besäte Land
ist aufgebrochen an euren Träumen—

In der Küche backt ihr Kuchen der Sara
denn immer wartet ein anderes draussen!—
Wiegt, was die Gründe vorgewogen haben

mischt, was von Gestirnen gemischt wurde
und was der Landmann ans Ende brachte.
Die Sehnsucht der Erde greift nach euch

mit dem Duff des geöffneten Gewürzschreines.
Die Dudaimbeere im Weizenfelde, die, seit Ruben
sie fand, ins Unsichtbare gewachsen war,

rötet sich wieder an eurer Liebe.

Women and girls of Israel

Women and girls of Israel,
the land sown with the bush of sleep
is broken open by your dreams—

In the kitchen you bake the cake of Sarah
for something else is always outside waiting!—
Weigh what reasons have weighed before

mix what was mixed by constellations
and what the yeoman completed.
The longing of earth reaches for you

with the scent of the opened shrine of spices.
Mandrake in the cornfield, which, since Reuben
found it, had grown into invisibility,

reddens again with your love.

Aber die Wüste, die grosse Wegwende zur
    Ewigkeit hin,
die mit ihrem Sande schon die Stundenuhr
der Mondzeit zu füllen begonnen hatte,

atmet über den verschütteten Fusspuren
der Gottgänger, und ihre verdorrten Quelladern
füllen sich mit Fruchtbarkeit—

denn euer Schatten, Frauen und Mädchen Israels,
strich über ihr brennendes Goldtopasgesicht
mit dem Frauensegen—

But the desert, the great bend in the road to eternity,
which had already begun to fill with its sand
the hourglass of lunar time,

breathes above the filled-in footsteps
of those who go to God, and its parched veined springs
fill with fertility—

for your shadow, women and girls of Israel,
swept across its golden topaz face
with the women's blessing—

—*Translated by Ruth and Matthew Mead*

Über den wiegenden Häuptern der Mütter

Über den wiegenden Häuptern der Mütter
öffnen sich zur Nachtzeit wieder
der Hirtengestirne Blütenzweige
singen in der Kinder warmen Schlaf
die ewigen Verwandlungen zu Gott hinein.
Die heimatlosen Jahrtausende
die seit dem Brande des Tempels umherirrten
ungeliebt in der Stundenuhr des Staubes
schlagen aus in neuer Herrlichkeit
in den Betten der Kinder
frische Äste überwinterter Bäume.

Above the rocking heads of the mothers

Above the rocking heads of the mothers
the blossom branches of the shepherds' stars
open again at night
singing in the warm sleep of children
the eternal transformations up to God.
The homeless millennia
which since the burning of the temple roamed about
unloved in the hourglass of dust
break forth in new glory
in the children's beds
fresh branches of the trees surviving winter.

—Translated by Ruth and Matthew Mead

Die ihr in den Wüsten

Die ihr in den Wüsten
verhüllte Quelladern sucht—
mit gebeugten Rücken
im Hochzeitslicht der Sonne lauscht—
Kinder einer neuen Einsamkeit mit Ihm—

Eure Fusspuren
treten die Sehnsucht hinaus
in die Meere aus Schlaf—
während euer Leib
des Schattens dunkles Blumenblatt auswirft
und auf neugeweihtem Land
das zeitmessende Zwiegespräch
zwischen Stern und Stern beginnt.

You who seek

You who seek hidden
veins of water in the desert—
listening with bent backs
in the nuptial light of the sun—
children of a new loneliness with Him—

Your footprints
tread longing
into the seas of sleep—
while your bodies
cast the shadow's dark petal
and on newly consecrated land
the time-measuring dialogue
between star and star begins.

O meine Mutter

O meine Mutter,
wir, die auf einem Waisenstern wohnen—
zu Ende seufzen den Seufzer derer
die in den Tod gestossen wurden—
wie oft weicht unter deinen Schritten der Sand
und lässt dich allein—

In meinen Armen liegend
kostest du das Geheimnis
das Elia bereiste—
wo Schweigen redet
Geburt und Sterben geschieht
und die Elemente anders gemischt werden—

Meine Arme halten dich
wie ein hölzerner Wagen die Himmelfahrenden—
weinendes Holz, ausgebrochen
aus seinen vielen Verwandlungen—

O my mother

O my mother,
we who dwell on an orphan star—
sighing to the end the sighs of those
who were thrust into death—
how often the sand gives way beneath your steps
and leaves you alone—

Lying in my arms
you taste the mystery
Elijah knew—
where silence speaks
birth and death occur
and the elements are mixed differently—

My arms hold you
as a wooden cart holds those ascending to heaven—
weeping wood, broken out
from its many transformations—

O meine Rückkehrerin,
das Geheimnis verwachsen mit Vergessenheit—
höre ich doch ein Neues
in deiner zunehmenden Liebe!

O you who return,
the mystery overgrown with forgetting—
I still hear something new
in your increasing love!

—*Translated by Ruth and Matthew Mead*

Du sitzt am Fenster

Du sitzt am Fenster
und es schneit—
dein Haar ist weiss
und deine Hände—
aber in den beiden Spiegeln
deines weissen Gesichts
hat sich der Sommer erhalten:
Land, für die ins Unsichtbare erhobenen Wiesen—
Tränke, für Schattenrehe zur Nacht.

Aber klagend sinke ich in deine Weisse,
deinen Schnee—
aus dem sich das Leben so leise entfernt
wie nach einem zu Ende gesprochenen Gebet—

O einzuschlafen in deinem Schnee
mit allem Leid im Feueratem der Welt.

Während die zarten Linien deines Hauptes
schon fortsinken in Meeresnacht
zu neuer Geburt.

You sit by the window

You sit by the window
and it is snowing—
your hair is white
and your hands—
but in both mirrors
of your white face
summer has been maintained:
Land for meadows raised into the invisible—
potions for shadow deer at night.

But mourning I sink into your whiteness,
your snow—
which life leaves ever so quietly
as after a prayer spoken to the end—

O to fall asleep in your snow
with all my grief in the fiery breath of the world.

While the delicate lines on your brow
drown already in the ocean of night
for a new birth.

—*Translated by Michael Roloff*

Wenn der Tag leer wird

Wenn der Tag leer wird
in der Dämmerung,
wenn die bilderlose Zeit beginnt,
die einsamen Stimmen sich verbinden—
die Tiere nichts als Jagende sind
oder gejagt—
die Blumen nur noch Duft—
wenn alles namenlos wird wie am Anfang—
gehst du unter die Katakomben der Zeit,
die sich auftun denen, die nahe am Ende sind
dort wo die Herzkeime wachsen—
in die dunkle Innerlichkeit hinab
sinkst du—
schon am Tode vorbei
der nur ein windiger Durchgang ist—
und schlägst frierend vom Ausgang
deine Augen auf
in denen schon ein neuer Stern
seinen Abglanz gelassen hat—

When day grows empty

When day grows empty
at dusk,
when the imageless time begins,
the lonely voices combine—
the animals are hunters only
or hunted—
the flowers mere fragrance—
when everything becomes nameless as at
    the beginning—
then you go beneath the catacombs of time
that open for those nearing the end—
there where the heart has its inception—
down into dark inwardness
you sink—
already past death
that is only a windy passage—
and freezing with exit
you open your eyes
in which a new star
already has left its reflection—

—*Translated by Michael Roloff*

Am Abend weitet sich dein Blick

Am Abend weitet sich dein Blick
sieht über Mitternacht hinaus—
doppelt bin ich vor dir—
grüne Knospe, die aus vertrocknetem Kelchblatt steigt,
in dem Zimmer darin wir zwei Welten angehören.
Du reichst auch schon weit über die Toten,
die hiesigen.
Weisst um das Aufgeblühte
ans der rätselumrindeten Erde.

Wie im Mutterleib das Ungeborene
mit dem Urlicht auf dem Hanpte
randlos sieht
von Stern zn Stern—
So fliesst Ende zum Anfang
wie ein Schwanenschrei.
Wir sind in einem Krankenzimmer.
Aber die Nacht gehört den Engeln!

In the evening your vision widens

In the evening your vision widens
looks out beyond midnight—
twofold I stand before you—
green bud rising out of dried-up sepal,
in the room where we are of two worlds.
You too already extend far beyond the dead,
those who are here,
and know of what has flowered
out of the earth with its bark of enigma.

As in the womb the unborn
with the primordial light on its brow
has the rimless view
from star to star—
So ending flows to beginning
like the cry of a swan.
We are in a sickroom.
But the night belongs to the angels.

—Translated by Michael Roloff

Aber in der Nacht

Aber in der Nacht,
wenn die Träume mit einem Luftzug
Wände und Zimmerdecken fortziehn,
beginnt die Wanderung zu den Toten.
Unter dem Sternstaub suchst du sie—

Deine Sehnsucht baut an der Schwester—
aus den Elementen, die sie verborgen halten,
holst du sie herein
bis sie aufatmet in deinem Bett—
der Bruder aber ist um die Ecke gegangen
und der Gatte zu hoch schon eingekehrt
da lässt die Demut dich verstummen—

Aber dann—wer hat die Reise unterbrochen—
beginnt die Rückkehr—
Wie der kleinen Kinder Wehklagen
erschrocken an der Erde
bist du—

But in the night

But in the night,
when dreams pull away
walls and ceilings with a breath of air,
the trek to the dead begins.
You search for them under the stardust—

Your longing builds up your sister—
from the elements which keep her hidden,
you bring her in
till she sighs with relief in your bed—
but your brother has gone round the corner
and your husband sits in too high a place
so that humility makes you silent—

But then—who has broken the journey—
the return begins—
like little children wailing
you are
frightened on the earth—

der Tod der Toten ist mit der Zimmerdecke
herabgesunken—
schützend liegt mein Kopf auf deinem Herzen
die Liebe—zwischen dir und dem Tod—

So kommt die Dämmerung
mit dem roten Sonnensamen hingestreut
und die Nacht hat sich ausgeweint
in den Tag—

the death of the dead has sunk down
with the ceiling—
my head lies on your heart protectingly
love—in between you and death—

Thus dawn comes
strewn with the red seed of the sun
and night has cried itself out
into the day—

—Translated by Ruth and Matthew Mead

Wohin O wohin

Wohin O wohin
du Weltall der Sehnsucht
das in der Raupe schon dunkel verzaubert
die Flügel spannt,
mit den Flossen der Fische
immer den Anfang beschreibt
in Wassertiefen, die
ein einziges Herz
ausmessen kann mit dem Senkblei
der Trauer.
Wohin o wohin
du Weltall der Sehnsucht
mit der Träume verlorenen Erdreichen
und der gesprengten Blutbahn des Leibes;
während die Seele zusammengefaltet wartet
auf ihre Neugeburt
unter dem Eis der Todesmaske.

Whither O whither

Whither O whither
you universe of longing
spreading your wings in the chrysalis
already darkly enchanted,
always describing the beginning
with the fins of fishes
in the watery depths which
a single heart
can sound with the plummet
of sorrow.
Whither O whither
you universe of longing
with the dreams of lost earths
and the burst vein of the body;
while the soul, folded, waits
to be born again
under the ice of the death mask.

—*Translated by Ruth and Matthew Mead*

Chassidische Schriften

*Es heisst: die Gebote der Thora entsprechen der Zahl
der Knochen des Menschen, ihre Verbote der Zahlder
    Adern.
So deckt das game Gesetz den ganzen Menschenleib.*

Alles ist Heil im Geheimnis
und das Wort lief aus
das atemverteilende Weltall,

schützt wie Masken mit seiner abgewandten Seite
die sternegebärende Nacht.

Alles ist Heil im Geheimnis
und lebendig aus der Quelle
wuchs die Sehnsucht

durch die Geschöpfe.
Namen bildeten sich
wie Teiche im Sand.

Hasidic Scriptures

It is said: the commandments of the Torah equal the number of a man's bones, its prohibitions the number of the veins. Thus the whole law covers the whole human body.

All is salvation in the mystery
and the word went forth
the breath-dispensing universe

protects like masks with its side turned away
the night giving birth to stars.

All is salvation in the mystery
and lively from the source
longing grew

through the creatures.
Names formed
like pools in the sand.

Alles ist Heil im Geheimnis
und die Knochen leben die magische Zahl der Gebote
und die Adern bluten sich zu Ende

wie Sonnenuntergang,
einmal übertretend die Gesetze im Schmerz.

Alles ist Heil im Geheimnis
und lebt aus der Erinnerung
und aus Vergessenheit graut der Tod.

Und die Bundeslade zog ihre Träger
über den Jordan, denn die Elemente trieben
geschwisterhaft die Segnung der Schrift!

Und das Herz der Steine,
flugsandangefüllt,
ist der Mitternächte Aufbewahrungsort
und der begrabenen Blitze Wohnstatt

Und Israel, der Horizontenkämpfer
schläft mit dem Sternensamen
und den schweren Träumen zu Gott!

All is salvation in the mystery
and the bones live the magic number of the command-
    ments
and the veins bleed to the end

like sunset,
transgressing once the laws of pain.

All is salvation in the mystery
and lives from memory
and death threatens from forgetfulness.

And the ark of the covenant drew its bearers
across the Jordan, for the elements drove
like kith and kin the blessing of the scripture!

And the heart of stones,
filled with quicksand,
is the place where midnights are stored up
and the dwelling place of buried lightning

And Israel, the fighter of horizons
sleeps with the seed of stars
and the heavy dreams towards God!

—*Translated by Ruth and Matthew Mead*

Zuweilen wie Flammen

Zuweilen wie Flammen
jagt es durch unseren Leib—
als wäre er verwoben noch mit der Gestirne
Anbeginn.

Wie langsam leuchten wir in Klarheit auf—

O nach wieviel Lichterjahren haben sich unsere
Hände gefaltet zur Bitte—
unsere Kniee sich gesenkt—
und aufgetan sich unsere Seele
zum Dank?

Rushing at times like flames

Rushing at times
like flames through our bodies—
as if they were still woven with the beginning
of the stars.

How slowly we flash up in clarity—

Oil, after how many lightyears have our hands
folded in supplication—
our knees bent—
and our souls opened
in thanks?

Wie Nebelwesen

Wie Nebelwesen
gehen wir durch Träume und Träume
Mauern von siebenfarbigem Licht
durchsinken wir—

Aber endlich farblos, wortlos
des Todes Element
im Kristallbecken der Ewigkeit
abgestreift aller Geheimnisse Nachtflügel…

Like beings of mist

Like beings of mist
we walk through dreams and dreams
we sink through walls
of seven-colored light—

But colorless at last, wordless
the element of death
in the crystal vessel of eternity
stripped off the nightwings of all mysteries...

—Translated by Ruth and Matthew Mead

Engel anf den Urgefilden

Engel auf den Urgefilden
die ilir den Anfang losbindet,
die Weissagungen in die Elemente sät
bis die Fruchtknoten der Gestirne
sich rönden
und wieder die Monde des Todes
die abnehmende Tonleiter singen—

Und in staubiger Nachtwache
der Mensch die Arme wild
zum Himmel wirft
und *Gott* sagt
und die Dunkelheit
in einer Veilchenträne duftet—

Engel auf den Urgefilden
wieviel Martermeilen
muss die Sehnsucht, zurück
zu eurem Segensraum durcheilen!

Angels upon the primeval fields

Angels upon the primeval fields
you who unbind the beginning,
sowing the prophecies into the elements
until the pistils of the constellations
round
and again the moons of death
sing down the scale—

And in the dusty nightwatch
man throws his arms wildly
up to heaven
and says *God*
and in the tear of a violet
the darkness smells—

Angels upon the primeval fields
how many tormented miles
must longing hurry back through
to your blessed space!

—*Translated by Ruth and Matthew Mead*

Wer weiß, welche magischen Handlungen

Wer weiss, welche magischen Handlungen
sich in den unsichtbaren Räumen vollziehn?

Wieviel glühende Rosen der Beschwörung
auf den Gewehrmündungen der Krieger blühn?

Welche Netze die Liebe knüpft
über einem bleichen Krankengesicht?

Manch einer hörte seinen Namen rufen
am Scheideweg

und kämpfte handlos in der Heiligen Scharen.
O die Brunnen, gebohrt in die Luft

daraus Prophetenwort trinkt,
und ein Staubvergrabener plötzlich seinen Durst löscht.

Welche Saaten an den Gestirnen des Blutes erwachsen
welche Missernten des Kummers.

Who knows what magic acts

Who knows what magic acts
occur in the invisible rooms?

How many glowing roses of invocation
bloom on the rifle barrels of the soldiers?

What nets love knots
above a pale sick face?

Many have heard their names called
where the road forks

and fought without hands in the company of saints.
O the wells, bored into the air,

from which words of prophets drink
and a man buried in dust suddenly quenches his thirst.

What seeds growing on the constellations of the blood
what tailed harvests of grief.

Und der Heiligen Lese aus Licht.
Ringmauern für die schwärzesten Taten.

Friedhöfe für die Martern
der bis auf den Gottgrund zerrissenen Opfer.

O die unsichtbaren Städte
darin die Schlafenden ihre Ausflüge machen—

Wälder der Traumgesichte—
was werdet ihr sein in Wahrheit nach unserem Tod?

And the saints' vintage of light.
Ramparts for the blackest deeds.

Cemeteries for the torments of
the victims torn to the very depth of God.

O the invisible cities
in which the sleepers make their excursions—

Forests of visions—
what will you be in truth after our death?

   —Translated by Ruth and Matthew Mead

Schmetterling

Welch schönes Jenseits
ist in deinen Staub gemalt.
Durch den Flammenkern der Erde,
durch ihre steinerne Schale
wurdest du gereicht,
Abschiedswebe in der Vergänglichkeken Mass.

Schmetterling
aller Wesen gute Nacht!
Die Gewichte von Leben und Tod
senken sich mit deinen Flügeln
auf die Rose nieder
die mit dem heimwärts reifenden Licht welkt.

Welch schönes Jenseits
ist in deinen Staub gemalt.
Welch Königszeichen
im Geheimnis der Luft.

Butterfly

What lovely aftermath
is painted in your dust.
You were led through the flaming
core of earth,
through its stony shell,
webs of farewell in the transient measure.

Butterfly
blessed night of all beings!
The weights of life and death
sink down with your wings
on the rose
which withers with the light ripening homewards.

What lovely aftermath
is painted in your dust.
What royal sign
in the secret of the air.

—*Translated by Ruth and Matthew Mead*

Musik in den Ohren der Sterbenden

Musik in den Ohren der Sterbenden—
Wenn die Wirbeltrommel der Erde
leise nachgewitternd auszieht—
wenn die singende Sehnsucht der fliegenden Sonnen,
die Geheimnisse deutungsloser Planeten
und die Wanderstimme des Mondes nach dem Tod
in die Ohren der Sterbenden fliessen,
Melodienkrüge füllend im abgezehrten Staub.

Staub, der offen steht zur seligen Begegnung,
Staub, der sein Wesen auffahren lässt,
Wesen, das sich einmischt in die Rede
der Engel und Liebenden—
und vielleicht schon eine dunkle Sonne
neu entzünden hilft—
denn alles stirbt sich gleich:
Stern und Apfelbaum
und nach Mitternacht
reden nur Geschwister—

Music in the ears of the dying

Music in the ears of the dying—
When the rolling drum of earth
takes the field soft as a dying storm—
when the singing desire of flying suns,
the secrets of meaningless planets
and the wandering voice of the moon after death
flow into the ears of the dying,
filling vessels of melody in the emaciated dust.

Dust, which stands open to blissful encounter,
Dust, that lets its being ascend,
Being, that mingles in the talk
of angels and lovers—
and is helping perhaps
to ignite anew
a dark sun—
for everything dies in the same way:
star and apple tree
and after midnight
only kith and kin speak—

—*Translated by Ruth and Matthew Mead*

Im Lande Israel

Nicht Kampfgesänge will ich euch singen
Geschwister, Ausgesetzte vor den Türen der Welt.
Erben der Lichterlöser, die aus dem Sande
autrissen die vergrabenen Strahlen
der Ewigkeit.
Die in ihren Händen hielten
funkelnde Gestirne als Siegestrophäen.

Nicht Kampflieder
will ich euch singen
Geliebte,
nur das Blut stillen
und die Tränen, die in Totenkammern gefrorenen,
auftauen.

In the Land of Israel

I do not want to sing you battle hymns,
brothers and sisters, outcasts standing before the doors
    of the world.
Heirs of the redeemers of light, who tore out of
    the sand
the buried rays
of eternity.
Who held in their hands
sparkling constellations as trophies of victory.

I do not
want to sing you battle songs,
beloved,
only stanch the blood
and thaw out the tears
which froze in the death chambers.

Und die verlorenen Erinnerungen suchen
die durch die Erde weissagend duften
und auf dem Stein schlafen
darin die Beete der Träume wurzeln
und die Heimwehleiter
die den Tod übersteigt.

And seek the lost memories
which smell prophetically through the earth
and sleep on the stone
in which root the flowerbeds of dreams
and the ladder of homesickness
which transcends death.

—Translated by Ruth and Matthew Mead

Völker der Erde

Völker der Erde
ihr, die ihr euch mit der Kraft der unbekannten
Gestirne umwickelt wie Garnrollen,
die ihr näht und wieder auftrennt das Genähte,
die ihr in die Sprachverwirrung steigt
wie in Bienenkörbe,
um im Süssen zu stechen
und gestochen zu werden—

Völker der Erde,
zerstöret nicht das Weltall der Worte,
zerschneidet nicht mit den Messern des Hasses
den Laut, der mit dem Atem zugleich geboren wurde.

Völker der Erde,
O dass nicht Einer Tod meine, wenn er Leben sagt—
und nicht Einer Blut, wenn er Wiege spricht—

Peoples of the earth

Peoples of the earth,
you who swathe yourselves with the force of
   the unknown
constellations as with rolls of thread,
you who sew and sever what is sewn,
you who enter the tangle of tongues
as into beehives,
to sting the sweetness
and be stung—

Peoples of the earth,
do not destroy the universe of words,
let not the knife of hatred lacerate
the sound born together with the first breath.

Peoples of the earth,
O that no one mean death when he says life—
and not blood when he speaks cradle—

Völker der Erde,
lasset die Worte an ihrer Quelle,
denn sie sind es, die die Horizonte
in die wahren Himmel rücken können
und mit ihrer abgewandten Seite
wie eine Maske dahinter die Nacht gähnt
die Sterne gebären helfen—

Peoples of the earth,
leave the words at their source,
for it is they that can nudge
the horizons into the true heaven
and that, with night gaping behind
their averted side, as behind a mask,
help give birth to the stars—

Wenn im Vorsommer

Wenn im Vorsommer der Mond geheime
   Zeichen aussendet,
die Kelche der Lilien Dufthimmel verströmen,
öffnet sich manches Ohr unter Grillengezirp
dem Kreisen der Erde und der Sprache
der entschränkten Geister zu lauschen.

In den Träumen aber fliegen die Fische in der Luft
und ein Wald wurzelt sich im Zimmerfussboden fest.

Aber mitten in der Verzauberung spricht
   eine Stimme klar und verwundert:
Welt, wie kannst du deine Spiele wetter spielen
und die Zeit betrügen—
Welt, man hat die kleinen Kinder wie Schmetterlinge,
flügelschlagend in die Flamme geworfen—

When in early summer

When in early summer the moon sends out secret signs,
the chalices of lilies scent of heaven,
some ear opens to listen
beneath the chirp of the cricket
to earth turning and the language of spirits set free.

But in dreams fish fly in the air
and a forest takes firm root in the floor of the room.

But in the midst of enchantment a voice speaks
    clearly and amazed:
World, how can you go on playing your games
and cheating time—
World, the little children were thrown like butterflies,
wings beating into the flames—

und deine Erde ist nicht wie ein fauler Apfel
in den schreckaufgejagten Abgrund
    geworfen worden—

Und Sonne und Mond sind waiter
    spazierengegangen—
zwei schieläugige Zeugen, die nichts gesehen haben.

and your earth has not been thrown like a rotten apple
into the terror-roused abyss—

And sun and moon have gone on walking—
two cross-eyed witnesses who have seen nothing.

—Translated by Ruth and Matthew Mead

Wir üben heute schon den Tod von morgen

Wir üben heute schon den Tod von morgen
wo noch das alte Sterben in uns welkt—
O Angst der Menschheit nicht zu überstehn—

O Todgewöhnung bis hinein in Träume
wo Nachtgerüst in schwarze Scherben fällt
und beinern Mond in den Ruinen leuchtet—

O Angst der Menschheit nicht zu überstehn—

Wo sind die sanften Rutengänger
Ruhe-Engel, die den verborgnen Quell
uns angerührt, der von der Müdigkeit
zum Sterben rinnt?

We rehearse tomorrow's death even today

We rehearse tomorrow's death even today
while the old dying still wilts within us—
O humanity's dread not to endure—

O death-accustoming down into dreams
where night scaffolding breaks into black fragments
and moon glows like bones on the ruins—

O humanity's dread not to endure—

Where are you, gentle dowsers,
peace angels that used to touch
the hidden source for us
that flows from weariness
into death.

—*Translated by Michael Roloff*

GREEN INTEGER
Pataphysics and Pedantry

Douglas Messerli, *Publisher*

Essays, Manifestos, Statements, Speeches, Maxims,
Epistles, Diaristic Notes, Narratives, Natural Histories,
Poems, Plays, Performances, Ramblings, Revelations
and all such ephemera as may appear necessary
to bring society into a slight tremolo of confusion
and fright at least.

*

Individuals may order Green Integer titles through PayPal
(www.Paypal.com). Please pay the price listed below plus $2.00 for
postage to Green Integer through the PayPal system.
You can also visit our site at www.greeninteger.com
If you have questions please feel free to e-mail the publisher at
info@greeninteger.com
Bookstores and libraries should order through our distributors:
USA and Canada: Consortium Book Sales and Distribution
1045 Westgate Drive, Suite 90, Saint Paul, Minnesota 55114-1065
United Kingdom and Europe: Turnaround Publisher Services
Unit 3, Olympia Trading Estate, Coburg Road, Wood Green,
London N22 6TZ UK

*

Andrée Chedid *Fugitive Suns: Selected Poetry*
[1-892295-25-3] $11.95
Anton Chekhov *A Tragic Man Despite Himself: The Complete
Short Plays* [1-931243-17-4] $24.95
Joseph Conrad *Heart of Darkness* [1-892295-49-0] $10.95
Charles Dickens *A Christmas Carol* [1-931243-18-2] $8.95
Mohammed Dib *L.A. Trip: A Novel in Verse* [1-931243-54-9] $11.95
Michael Disend *Stomping the Goyim* [1-9312243-10-7] $12.95
±José Donoso *Hell Has No Limits* [1-892295-14-8] $10.95
Oswald Egger *Room of Rumor: Tunings* [1-931243-66-2] $9.95
Andreas Embiricos *Amour Amour* [1-931243-26-3] $11.95
Ford Madox Ford *The Good Soldier* [1931243-62-x] $10.95
Jean Frémon •*Island of the Dead* [1-931243-31-x] $12.95
Sigmund Freud [with Wilhelm Jensen] *Gradiva* and *Delusion
and Dream in Wilhelm Jensen's* Gradiva
[1-892295-89-x] $13.95
Federico García Lorca *Suites* 1-892295-61-x] $12.95
Dieter M. Gräf *Tousled Beauty* [1-933382-01-5] $11.95
Elana Greenfield *Damascus Gate: Short Hallucinations*
[1-931243-49-2] $10.95
Jean Grenier *Islands: Lyrical Essays* [1-892295-95-4] $12.95
Barbara Guest *The Confetti Trees* [Sun & Moon Press:
1-55713-390-5] $10.95
Hagiwara Sakutarō *Howling at the Moon: Poems and Prose*
[1-931243-01-8] $11.95
Joshua Haigh [Douglas Messerli] *Letters from Hanusse*
[1-892295-30-x] $12.95
†Knut Hamsun *The Last Joy* [1-931243-19-0] $12.95
On Overgrown Paths [1-892295-10-5] $12.95
A Wanderer Plays on Muted Strings
[1-893395-73-3] $10.95

Sigurd Hoel *Meeting at the Milestone* [1-892295-31-8] $15.95

Hsu Hui-chih *Book of Reincarnation* [1-931243-32-8] $9.95

Vicente Huidobro *Manifestos Manifest* [1-892295-08-3] $12.95

Wilhelm Jensen [with Sigmund Freud] *Gradiva* and *Delusion and Dream in Wilhelm Jensen's* Gradiva [1-893395-89-x] $12.95

James Joyce *On Ibsen* [1-55713-372-7] $8.95

Richard Kalich *Charlie P* [1-933382-05-8] $12.95

Ko Un *Ten Thousand Lives* [1-933382-06-6] $14.95

Alexei Kruchenykh *Suicide Circus: Selected Poems* [1-892295-27-x] $12.95

Else Lasker-Schüler *Selected Poems* [1-892295-86-5] $11.95

Mario Luzi *Earthly and Heavenly Journey of Simone Martini* [1-9312433-53-0] $14.95

†Thomas Mann *Six Early Stories* [1-892295-74-1] $10.95

†Harry Martinson *Views from a Tuft of Grass* [1-931243-78-6] $10.95

Julio Matas [with Carlos Felipe and Virgilio Piñera] *Three Masterpieces of Cuban Drama* [1-892295-66-0] $12.95

±Friederike Mayröcker *with each clouded peak* [Sun & Moon Press: 1-55713-277-1] $11.95

Deborah Meadows *Representing Absence* [1-931243-77-8] $9.95

Douglas Messerli *After* [Sun & Moon Press: 1-55713-353-0] $10.95

Bow Down [ML&NLF: 1-928801-04-8] $12.95

First Words [1-931243-41-7] $10.95

ed. *Listen to the Mockingbird: American Folksongs and Popular Music Lyrics of the 19th Century* [1-892295-20-2] $13.95

Maxims from My Mother's Milk/Hymns to Him: A Dialogue [Sun & Moon Press: 1-55713-047-7] $8.95 [ed. with Mac Wellman]

From the Other Side of the Century: A New American Drama 1960-1995
[Sun & Moon Press: 1-55713-274-x] $29.95
see also Joshua Haigh and Kier Peters

Sheila E. Murphy *Letters to Unfinished J.* [1-931243-59-x] $10.95

Gellu Naum *My Tired Father / Pohem* [1-892295-07-5] $8.95

Murat Nemet-Nejat *The Peripheral Space of Photography*
[1-892295-90-3] $9.95

Vítězslav Nezval •*Antilyrik & Other Poems* [1-892295-75-x] $10.95

Henrik Nordbrandt *The Hangman's Lament: Poems*
[1-931243-56-5] $10.95

John O'Keefe *The Deatherians* [1-931243-50-6] $10.95

Toby Olson *Utah* [1-892295-35-0] $12.95

OyamO *The Resurrection of Lady Lester* [1-892295-51-2] $8.95

Kier Peters *A Dog Tries to Kiss the Sky: 7 Short Plays*
[1-931243-30-1] $12.95

The Confirmation [Sun & Moon Press:
1-55713-154-6] $6.95

Pedro Pietri *The Masses Are Asses* [1-892295-62-8] $8.95

Edgar Allan Poe *Eureka, A Prose Poem* [1-55713-329-8] $10.95

Jean Renoir *An Interview* [1-55713-330-1] $9.95

Rainer Maria Rilke *Duino Elegies* [1-931243-07-7] $10.95

Reina María Rodríguez *Violet Island and Other Poems*
[1-892295-65-2] $12.95

Martha Ronk *Displeasures of the Table* [1-892295-44-x] $9.95

Joe Ross *EQUATIONS=equals* [1-931243-61-1] $10.95

Amelia Rosselli *War Variations* [1-931243-55-7] $14.95

Tiziano Rossi *People on the Run* [1-931243-37-9] $12.95

Arno Schmidt *Radio Dialogs I* [1-892295-01-6] $12.95

Radio Dialogs II [1-892295-80-6] $13.95

Oscar Wilde *The Critic As Artist* [1-55713-328-x] $9.95
William Carlos Williams *The Great American Novel*
                              [1-931243-52-2] $10.95
Yang Lian *Yi* [1-892295-68-7] $14.95
Yi Ch'ōngjun *Your Paradise* [1-931243-69-7] $13.95
Visar Zhiti *The Condemned Apple: Selected Poetry*
                              [1-931243-72-7] $10.95

† Author winner of the Nobel Prize for Literature
± Author winner of the America Award for Literature
• Book translation winner of the PEN American Center
  Translation Award [PEN-West]
* Book translation winner of the PEN/Book-of-the-Month Club
  Translation Prize
+ Book translation winner of the PEN Award for Poetry in
  Translation

The America Awards

FOR A LIFETIME CONTRIBUTION TO INTERNATIONAL WRITING

Awarded by the Contemporary Arts Educational Project, Inc.
in loving memory of Anna Fahrni

The 2007 Award winner is:

PAAVO HAAVIKKO

[Finland] 1931

Previous winners:

1994 AIMÉ CESAIRE [Martinique] 1913
1995 HAROLD PINTER [England] 1930
1996 JOSÉ DONOSO [Chile] 1924-1996 (awarded prior to his death)
1997 FRIEDERIKE MAYRÖCKER [Austria] 1924
1998 RAFAEL ALBERTI [Spain] 1902-1998 (awarded prior to his death)
1999 JACQUES ROUBAUD [France] 1932
2000 EUDORA WELTY [USA] 1909-2001
2001 INGER CHRISTENSEN [Denmark] 1935
2002 PETER HANDKE [Austria] 1942
2003 ADONIS [Syria/Lebanon] 1930
2004 JOSÉ SARAMAGO [Portugal] 1922
2005 ANDREA ZANZOTTO [Italy] 1921
2006 JULIEN GRACQ (Louis Poirier) [France] 1910

The rotating panel for The America Awards currently consists of Douglas Messerl [chairman], Will Alexander, Luigi Ballerini, Charles Bernstein, Peter Constantine Peter Glassgold, Deborah Meadows, Martin Nakell, John O'Brien, Marjorie Perloff Dennis Phillips, Joe Ross, Jerome Rothenberg, Paul Vangelisti, and Mac Wellman.